HERITAGE SERIES 3

"Stumbling Toward Maturity"

by

Arnold Theodore Olson

THE EVANGELICAL FREE CHURCH OF AMERICA

FREE CHURCH PRESS
901 East 78th Street
Minneapolis, MN 55420

Every effort has been made to identify and acknowledge the source of material used. If additional
information is obtained, it will be included in subsequent editions.

ISBN 0-911802-50-9
LIBRARY OF CONGRESS CATALOG NUMBER: 81-66943

Printed in the United States of America
by Free Church Press, Minneapolis, MN 55423

To Denise and Diana

Preface

𝐔he launching of the Free Church may be considered a result of daring rather than deliberate planning. Humanly speaking, the founders seem to have stumbled into the work. They stumbled into a movement which in a few years they absorbed with telling success. By the grace of God they were, however, divinely ordained to lead a new movement into larger fields and greater activities." So it seemed to those who prepared the Fiftieth Anniversary book of the then Swedish Evangelical Free Church.

This does not mean to imply that the founders were men of limited knowledge, although the Scriptures took priority as a textbook. One insisted that all a preacher needed was his Bible from which he got the message, an almanac to tell him when it was Sunday and how the weather would be in planning his itinerary, and a clock to tell him when it was time to begin the meeting. When to close was not important since that was "entirely in the hands of the Holy Spirit."

It should be noted that the leaders in the 1880s were also well-trained men. J. G. Princell of the Swedish Evangelical Free Church studied at the University of Chicago, majoring in Latin, Greek, and mathematics and at the German American College of Philadelphia. R. A. Jernberg, one of the founders of the Norwegian-Danish Evangelical Free Church Association, was a graduate of Yale University and the Chicago Theological Seminary. However, there were others who, though having acquired little secular knowledge, were men and women blessed with divine wisdom and a constantly expanding acquaintance with the Word of God. The early immigrants, who met Christ before emigrating to America from Scandinavia, were products of the Readers' Movement.

Even so, the new converts were literally babes in Christ. They were surrounded by people from the State Churches whose limited knowledge of Christianity had been taught by government appointed clergy and based on the interpretation by church leaders. As the new converts began to study the Scriptures they enjoyed a new freedom. The question was no longer, "What does the catechism say?" but "Where is it written in the Word?" This created problems calling for much soul-searching and further examination of the Book of Books. There was an immaturity which revealed itself in questions as to life style, relationship to the Church and her doctrines and the relationship of believers to one another as well as to non-believers. Answers to these questions were complicated by the absence of models, for all were "babes" in the beginning.

The problems faced by the new believers collectively were also related to this lack of maturity. This we have sought to cover in the first volume of this series, *The Search For Identity*. While some of the founders were well-educated, their understanding of life styles, doctrines and church structure was no less limited than among other new converts. All had known only the one Church, the Lutheran State Church of Denmark, Norway or Sweden. Was departure from the faith and practice of that church an apostasy? What were the signs of spiritual growth based on the new light coming from the Holy Spirit through the Bible?

The purpose of this volume is to deal with the spiritual growth of the individual believer and the collective growth within each congregation as well as of the denomination. It would be difficult to separate the two at times because the extent of the maturity of her members determines to a large degree the maturity of the congregation. The Scriptures refer to both—sometimes in the same passage.

And he gave some, apostles; and some, prophets; and some, evangelists; and some, pastors and teachers;
For the perfecting of the saints, for the work of the ministry, for the edifying of the body of Christ:
Till we all come in the unity of the faith, and of the knowledge of the Son of God, unto a perfect man, unto the measure of the stature of the fulness of Christ:
That we henceforth be no more children, tossed to and fro, and carried about with every wind of doctrine, by the sleight of men, and cunning craftiness, whereby they lie in wait to deceive;
But speaking the truth in love, may grow up into him in all things, which is the head, even Christ:
From whom the whole body fitly joined together and compacted by that which every joint supplieth, according to the effectual working in the measure of every part, maketh increase of the body unto the edifying of itself in love (Eph. 4:11-16).

*   *   *   *   *   *

Wherefore laying aside all malice, and all guile, and hypocrisies, and envies, and all evil speakings,
As newborn babes, desire the sincere milk of the word, that ye may grow thereby:
If so be ye have tasted that the Lord is gracious.
To whom coming, as unto a living stone, disallowed indeed of men, but chosen of God, and precious,
Ye also, as lively stones, are built up a spiritual house, an holy priesthood, to offer up spiritual sacrifices, acceptable to God by Jesus Christ (I Peter 2:1-5).

*   *   *   *   *   *

Now therefore ye are no more strangers and foreigners, but fellowcitizens with the saints, and of the household of God;
And are built upon the foundation of the apostles and prophets, Jesus Christ himself being the chief cornerstone;
In whom all the building fitly framed together groweth unto an holy temple in the Lord:
In whom ye also are builded together for an habitation of God

through the Spirit (Eph. 2:19-22).

*   *   *   *   *   *

And I, brethren, could not speak unto you as unto spiritual,
but as unto carnal, even as unto babes in Christ.
I have fed you with milk, and not with meat: for hitherto ye
were not able to bear it, neither yet now are ye able.
For ye are yet carnal: for whereas there is among you envying,
and strife, and divisions, are ye not carnal, and walk as men?
(I Cor. 3:1-4).

The imagery may vary, but the meaning is the same
whether using the illustration of a body or a building. The
growth is not so much a matter of statistics as it is spiritual
maturity. Carnality is equated with failure to move
beyond infancy.

The call is for a balanced maturity. In life some people
reach full physical adulthood but remain children in in-
tellect. There are others whose physical growth may be
stunted but whose minds border on genius. Likewise,
there are believers who, though Christians for years, never
seem to grow beyond the bottle and spoon-fed stage.
Others appear to increase rapidly in knowledge but are
unable to put it to practical use. There are congregations
fully grown in organization and sensitive to a well-stated
system of doctrine, but without spiritual life. A few
groups, spiritually alive but without a growing body die,
once the members of the fellowship join the Church
Triumphant. Some older and mature congregations suffer
from hardening of the spiritual arteries so that growth
slows down and even stops due to the absence of spiritual
renewals.

Scripture sometimes uses the word *perfection* to imply a
balanced growth, as noted in the expression "for the perfecting of the saints." Several of the newer translations use
the word *maturity* rather than *perfection.*

Therefore leaving the elementary teaching about the Christ,

let us press on to maturity, not laying again a foundation of repentance from dead works and of faith toward God, of instruction about washings, and laying on of hands, and the resurrection of the dead, and eternal judgment. And this we shall do, if God permits (Heb. 6:1-3 NAS).

This volume, however, will not endeavor to present an in-depth study of the Scriptural signs of maturity or lack thereof. It is rather a collection of stories and personal experiences which occurred as the denomination developed from a number of isolated outposts whose members were not only seeking God's will for new believers, but struggling with a new and strange culture and language. Some of the stories are humorous and others sad. There are sections on such subjects as life styles, language problems and the crystallization of doctrine. Many of the stories, some of which are autobiographical, could have served as illustrations in the first two volumes of the *Heritage Series,* but I thought it might be more interesting to put them all together in a separate one.

There are stories of honest mistakes and accidents which turned out to be providential. Throughout there is evidence of a movement toward maturity. We can write about the growth as Williston Walker wrote about the American Congregational Church: "It is a history of strength and of weakness, of apprehensions of divine truth and of occasional mistakes. The history of intermingling forces of the human and the divine in the unfolding of the Kingdom of God on earth must ever be so. But the story has been told to little purpose if two essential features of Congregational life have not appeared—those of unity and growth."*

---

*Walker, Williston, *The Creeds and Platforms of Congregationalism,* Pilgrim Press, Boston, 1893, p. 582.

Contents

Chapter I

TWO MOTHER TONGUES

Immigrants to America from the Scandinavian countries naturally sought churches of the Lutheran faith connected with the State Churches in the countries from which they had emigrated primarily because the old country languages were used. This was true even for those who had been touched by the revival movements in their homelands. But that was only the first and, for some, a temporary stop. Eventually, Bible study groups were started and met first in private homes. These developed into loosely organized Mission Societies and finally into congregations composed not only of those who were believers upon their arrival, but scores converted in the revivals sweeping across the Scandinavian immigrant communities. All groups had one thing in common, be it in the Lutheran Church, the Bible study groups, the Mission Society, or in the newly organized congregations of believers, and that was the Danish, Norwegian or Swedish language.

Some of the first English words learned had nothing to do with religious activity, but rather with the secular. These usually were, "Have you got a job?" and "How much pay?" The religious and social life was experienced in the mother tongue, but this was not because of an unwillingness to conform to the culture of the new land. In fact, they started at the earliest opportunity to learn English. After all, they had come to stay. I well remember how as a lad I would accompany my father to evening school English classes. He enrolled so as to qualify for

American citizenship as soon as legally possible. Later, my mother did the same. She wanted to vote in the elections! At home, I would read from a list of words for my father to pronounce, spell and pronounce again. How he struggled. It was done with a sense of companionship then and recalled with a sense of pride now. Upon receiving his final papers, he celebrated by providing us all with large portions of ice cream, a rare treat.

In 1884 a study of Scandinavian immigrants was made by home missionaries of the American Congregational Home Missions Society and workers for the American Sunday School Union to determine a program for a missionary activity among them and provide background material for Marcus Montgomery prior to a visit to Scandinavia to study the revival movement and its relation to congregationalism. The greater part of that report appears in *The Search For Identity.* One brief section bears repeating in this context:

> This republic—the hope and inspiration of the world—has nothing to fear from Scandinavians, but very much to gain. After a careful observation of these people in this land and in their native countries, I am clearly of the opinion that *they are more nearly like Americans than are any other foreign people.* In manners and customs, political and religious instincts, fertility of adaptation, personal appearance, and cosmopolitan character, they are strikingly like native Americans. No peculiar physiognomy is stamped upon them to point them out the world over; they find the English language easy, and quickly acquire it and lose their own brogue. The first generation of American-born Scandinavians, when they reach the age of twenty years, cannot generally be distinguished from Americans by either appearance, language, or customs.[1]

One wonders what the ultimate results will be in the United States once the practice of yielding to the demands of today's foreign language speaking minorities that children of today's immigrants be taught all subjects in the language of their parents in the American public schools and often by teachers who are themselves more adept in the use of Spanish, for example, than in the use of English. One prominent historian has predicted a splintering of the American communities at the very time they are seeking to wipe out racial divisions. Bilingualism has already polarized many communities. The melting pot would thus become a mosaic. My generation, the first born on this side of the Atlantic, was taught some of the language and culture of the lands of the immigrant parents, but that was done in special classes (usually during the summer) sponsored by the churches. On the other hand, though the early immigrants settled in communities for the Germans, Italians, Irish, Swedes, etc., they learned the language of America. Yet, when it came to the religious life they wished to worship in the mother tongue, for that was the way it had been from childhood. To wait until the members of the immigrant community could all understand and speak the new language would be to deprive them of years of Bible study, etc. It must be noted that they were not taught a second language in Europe as they are now.

The language was the language of prayer, praise and of their Bibles. It was also the language of their theology. Such terms as atonement, redemption or justification held no meaning to them. In fact, they were even unpronounceable. Scandinavian was also the channel of communication with fellow immigrants. Some were from the same village across the sea, for it was a common practice for immigrants from the same place to gravitate to the same settlements in the new world. Here they would not only worship together but share the latest news from the old country, for almost every week found recently arrived newcomers.

There was another important reason for establishing religious centers where the Scandinavian language was used. It was a time of revival. The unconverted had to be reached with the message of salvation before Christ's return. There was an urgency about it. One could not wait until the new arrivals learned English before confronting them with the invitation to Christ, the Savior. Itinerant evangelists would seek out those who understood the old country languages. This was also true among other ethnic groups such as the Dutch, Germans, Italians and now the Spanish.

The first generation of Evangelical Free Church people born in America were brought up in Swedish and Norwegian-Danish speaking congregations. There were many frustrations, especially among school teachers in predominently Scandinavian communities, when the children who spoke English in class, shifted to Scandinavian once they got outside the classroom. They would often in their games take advantage of those who understood only English. It became a secret code.[2]

As time went on, that first, and more so the second generation began to rebel against continuing church services in Scandinavian. The period of transition became one of the most difficult and even divisive periods in the history of the older congregations and also in denominational affairs.

One must try to understand the feelings of the pioneers as they stumbled toward maturity. For some, the new language was learned with great difficulty and then mixed with words from the mother tongue and expressed in a brogue betraying even the location of the community from which they had emigrated. They had worked hard and sacrificed much to build churches in which they might feel at home. One congregation had it written into the constitution that the purpose of the church organization was to "minister to the Norwegians and to the heathens." The heathens, of course, would be on fields abroad with no possibility of those converts coming to America seeking membership. In these churches they had witnessed the conversion of many of their *landsmenn* and for decades had prayed and worked together in the church. Their own children, too, had been converted in spite of the services being held in Scandinavian. Was all of this now to be taken away from them by a generation of their own children who, though knowing the God of their fathers, did not appreciate the inflexibility as to language. How about the new converts and transferees who had joined since the congregation had become bilingual? Would these now, in taking over the leadership, drop the Scandinavian, leaving the remaining pioneers with no place to go?

There were a number of reasons for the diminishing need for Scandinavian. First, there was a decrease in the number of new immigrants, and some of those who did come knew some English. Second, children of the pioneers who met and married other Americans who did not understand Scandinavian were often reluctant to break away from the fellowship. They valued their heritage and wanted their children to have the privilege of growing up in the same spiritual climate, but in their own language. Third, the pioneers wanted the best in education for their children, but providing for this contributed to their own problem. The offspring found it increasingly difficult, even irritating, to come from schools and churches where all was in English, only to find no change at home. Fourth, the evangelistic fervor of the pioneers inevitably contributed to the conversion of neighbors and fellow workers at the shop or in the office. Youth groups working in English but in the Scandinavian churches attracted other young people. For example, one congregation which worshipped entirely in Swedish and was inflexible on that score, sponsored a series of evangelistic services in a rented auditorium in town with the renowned Gustav F. Johnson as evangelist. The services were in English. A revival broke out, resulting in many conversions. Now the congregation was in a dilemma. Should it break down the language barrier to accommodate the new converts? This they did but not without seriously dividing the flock. The new converts contributed much to the work of the denomination—one pastor, one lay leader, and a woman active in the work of the Women's Missionary Society.

Other congregations which refused to recognize changes in cultural and linguistic environment went out of existence. A Salvation Army officer told me of visiting one such church with his wife one Sunday morning, only to find three people present—an elderly lady was the entire audience; another was at the organ while the pastor led the singing, gestures and all. The size of the audience did not dampen his enthusiasm. On seeing the couple entering, he excused himself to his one person audience and went down from the platform to greet the guests. The pastor was one of the few who refused to apply himself to learning English and this church was one of the few left open to him. The church was closed shortly thereafter. Such was not common. It must be said out of respect for the pastors, many succeeded in shifting to English. A few, though they worked hard at it, could not overcome a pronounced brogue—which today might be considered distingushed. Some retired early, while others turned to secular employment.

Another congregation was breathing its last when I visited it in the early 1940s. I found a few elderly women in attendance who had worked as maids in the homes of the wealthy. There were no families and the pastor supported himself by selling cleaning products house-to-house. This group was resuscitated by the arrival of a new group of immigrants who knew some English before leaving Norway. Attracted to the church because it was Norwegian, they nevertheless, though slowly, turned to the use of English. Today, it is a healthy congregation.

To the credit of many congregations, they became aware of the trends and sought to find ways to meet the challenge by arranging for bilingual congregations during the transition. A few, however, refused to face reality and defended their inflexibility by declaring themselves loyal to the commitment of the founders; namely, to serve the Scandinavian community even when there were none left!

Karl Olsson, the historian of the Evangelical Covenant Church, in writing of the language problem in that denomination noted:

> Even more strenuous efforts were made to keep the second generation properly oriented. Together with other immigrant churches, the Mission Friends decided to encourage the so-called "Swede school," an extra-curricular program which kept the children busy after school, or on Saturday, and frequently during the summer months. A theological student was often engaged to induct the young Swedish-Americans into the impossible pronounciation and tortuous syntax of the language of "honor and heroes." Much of this had ultimate value. It enriched the culture and linguistic perception of the children and gave them some understanding of the world-view of their parents. But as a measure of maintaining the character of the church, it was futile and perhaps even harmful. It gave the children a parochially narrow view of the church of Christ, and it did not serve to universalize the Covenant ideal. If the first generation had devoted as much time and energy to learning English as they spent on teaching their children Swedish, the Covenant would have been ready earlier to carry its message to the American community . . . The battle for the second generation became largely a linguistic one . . . In most places the language controversy was embittered. It was a true battle of the generations with all the complications of intimate loves and hatreds.[3]

Many were the complaints, some written for the annual reports to conferences. The following is an example:

> In other places the language problem is difficult . . . *Forbundets ungdomstidning* (the youth periodical first published in 1911) should have come out fifteen to twenty years ago . . . If we do not make a substantial effort . . . to preserve the Swedish language, matters will move so rapidly that we shall not be able to keep pace. In too many places we are about to lose the Swedish. We must quite simply use English to make Swedish understandable for our youth.
>
> Our main task now is to get our mission ideas and our pietistic principles into the English language. If our young people do

not hear English among us, they will go to the American churches. These have already swallowed too many of the children of the Mission Friends.[4]

The Salem Evangelical Free Church of Chicago was a pacesetter in meeting the problem. The building on the one corner housed a growing Norwegian congregation. However, leaders and people, concerned for their children and others in the community, reorganized the congregation, creating two departments under one board divided into two committees. In 1924 a building for an English department was erected on the next corner with parsonages for two pastors in between. This proved an answer to the problem for several years, but time does not stop. Today, the main, original structure is still in use for services in Spanish and English. The grandchildren of the Norwegian immigrants have long since scattered to the suburbs and many have been active in founding and supporting new Evangelical Free Church congregations.

Another example of churches facing the necessity of doing something about the language question occurred among the Swedes in Minneapolis. One of the original (1884) congregations of the Swedish Evangelical Free Church of America was located two blocks from another Swedish speaking congregation which was first organized as an independent church and called the Swedish Temple (1895), then reorganized in 1897 as the Swedish Congregational Temple. In 1926 the two congregations merged to form two departments under the leadership of two pastors. The older building was used for Swedish, and the Temple, two blocks away, for English. For reasons not pertinent to this story the arrangement, though noble in concept, lasted only three years when a division took place resulting in one part keeping the name of the temporarily united group, the First Evangelical Free Church; and the other adopting the name, Central Free Church.

Other churches tried, quite successfully, having two departments in the same building with simultaneous services. These were usually served by two pastors with the leader of the English program not necessarily familiar with any of the Scandinavian languages. This was true of both the Second Evangelical and the Norwegian Evangelical Free Church of Brooklyn. Others arranged for two services led by a bilingual pastor, with the morning worship in Scandinavian and the Sunday evening service in English. This was my experience as pastor of one congregation. As a teenager I led services in the lower auditorium of my home church while Norwegian was used in the sanctuary. Guest speakers were arranged by the Board of Deacons. I had to be prepared, however, to fill in the speaker's time in case he or she failed to show.

Gradually these forward looking congregations converted entirely to English, though a few may still conduct programs in Scandinavian on special occasions. The one remaining exception is at the Evangelical Free Church in Brooklyn. Eventually, the congregation was able to secure an adjacent building suitable for the English department which had been meeting in the lower auditorium of the main church structure. After a few years this satisfactory arrangement had to face a new problem, not related to language but still to progress. The city of New York wanted the land for a new highway approach to a bridge planned to cross the narrows of the harbor between Brooklyn and Staten Island. The city arranged for a plot a couple of blocks away but on the same thoroughfare. Two almost identical structures were erected at right angles to each other with one main entrance and lobby serving both. Both departments are active and unique among the congregations (1980).

There were also a few, fortunately very few, that stumbled and were even bruised in the struggle towards maturity. The issue of converting to a bilingual congregation in one church created a schism because the majority insisted on "everything in Norwegian." Those who were denied even a little English in the program withdrew with great reluctance and much bitterness to form a separate congregation. This did not solve the problem permanently. A new generation forced the original congregation to change to English. There followed the arrival of another group of immigrants who wanted Norwegian, but it was too late to turn the clock back, resulting in the formation of a third congregation—all Norwegian—in the same vicinity.

It must be noted that the one congregation which was slower in converting had good success in indoctrinating its youth in the Scriptures. The Sunday School and confirmation classes were conducted in Norwegian. Neighboring churches could well have taken notice of the importance of thorough teaching irrespective of language. That church has produced a college president, several pastors, a district superintendent and missionaries in spite of its inflexibility in language. Some of the leaders would justify the refusal to change by pointing to these results. In conversations with a number of the youth of that period who are now themselves grandparents, we discovered one weakness in the insistence by their parents that the Bible be taught in Norwegian. The young people in entering high school, college and American society experienced frustration as they tried to share their Christian faith with non-believers and discuss Christianity with believers. They could not communicate the Gospel as readily as they would have had they learned the English terminology at the time they were taught.

I was a member of the first American born generation in the Evangelical Free Church and sat (or was it slept) through many long Norwegian services and even longer after-meetings. It was a time of revival and many immigrants knelt at the altar. The impression was that English was the language at school and at play, a mixture of the two were the languages of the home, and Norwegian the language of religion. In other words, we spoke English Monday through Friday, mixed things up on Saturday and used Norwegian on Sunday! That was the language of good, sound, true Christianity. I remember being told on one occasion that at the next evening service a man who had been converted through the prision ministry of a Gospel team from the church would give his testimony. I was really excited, having never seen an ex-convict, much less heard one speak. I listened attentively to his story but went home confused and doubting the trustworthiness of his testimony. How could one be really saved if he was unable to confess Christ in Norwegian! It marked the first time I heard English spoken from the pulpit. Even the recitations by the children at Christmas were in Norwegian.

The first Bible course in English at the denominational seminary was not introduced until 1921. When I enrolled in 1927 I discovered to my dismay that Systematic Theology, a major requirement, was taught in Norwegian. The lecture outlines provided by the professor were also in Norwegian. All the others in the class were either Norwegian or Danish immigrants. It is a sad fact of history that the Free Church movement lost a generation of future pastors and potential denominational leaders at a most crucial time in the history of the church. Other denominations and institutions reaped the benefits. These young men took with them some of our outstanding women, as well, to be their wives. As a concession to the one young American in the class, I was permitted to answer oral questions and write the exams and dissertations in English.

I was called to my first parish with the understanding that all the activities, should I accept the call, would be in English, including the Adult Bible Class which traditionally had been in Norwegian and taught by the pastor. The inability to secure bilingual pastors in the 1940s hastened the shift to all English in many churches. All went well for me from April to Christmas (1930) at which time I received, as a Christmas gift from the adult class, a Norwegian Bible. In February I discovered the class was motivated by more than the Christmas spirit in presenting the Bible. I was asked if I was ready yet to preach in Norwegian. In response to much pressure, a Sunday was set for a first attempt. Preparation was long and tedious. First, the sermon was written, then mailed to a young lady, an expert in both languages who had minored in Norse history, literature and language at the University of Minnesota, for correction of grammar and vocabulary and returned to me to be memorized before delivery. It had one factor in its favor—the sermon was much shorter than usual, which must have been an act of mercy by reducing the time of suffering! Thereafter, Sunday morning services in Norwegian were held once every three months with the same procedure as followed in the first sermon. By the time I assumed the second pastorate, services in Norwegian were conducted every Sunday morning for a few years. However, we no longer had to use the postman since by then the editor of the sermons in Norwegian as well as of all my writings had become my wife. On our twenty-fifth wedding anniversary tour of Norway, the Oslo press reported that both of us spoke excellent Norwegian, but with an American accent. So the tables had turned after fifty years of hearing English spoken with a Scandinavian accent. After two weeks of touring and preaching, a Bergen newspaper observed with surprise and pride that we "both spoke fluent Norwegian." The reason for pride was the fact that my wife's parents had emigrated to America from Bergen. So we apparently lost our accent in two weeks. Difficult though the years of seeking to accommodate the elderly were, there was a great satisfaction in sensing the added blessing that was experienced in hearing the Word of God taught in the mother tongue. Just the ability to read the Bible and pray, however haltingly, in the language at the bedside of those nearing the end of life's journey brought its own reward. But the final abandonment of the Scandinavian language was inevitable. Many are the stories coming out of the transition period.

One congregation I served had begun a satellite work where I would preach on Sunday afternoons. An elderly lady was furious because the new pastor did not conduct the services in Norwegian. She would read from the Norwegian hymnal in a rather loud whisper throughout the sermon. Members of the congregation, considering the source, were very patient in not allowing the disturbance to hamper their own attention to the message. One Sunday, things became quiet. I wondered if she was ill. After the service she came to me with great enthusiasm saying, *"Tak for fisken"* (Thanks for the fish). I was puzzled for I had not made any reference to fish but she continued, *"Guds naade, saa velsignet"* (God's grace, so blessed). Then I recalled that in the sermon I had inadvertently used the Norwegian word for grace. From then on, early in the service I would toss her a fish in the form of a meaningful word such as redemption, forgiveness, heaven, etc. She would enjoy meditating on that word. Fortunately, she had a limited vocabulary. Others are more difficult to feed even with all the five loaves and two fishes.

During the transition period a few pastors maneuvered in many ways to postpone the completion of the changeover. For example, in one district an eight-day summer conference was held annually in Norwegian until pressure from the younger people forced the program committee to arrange for one day in English. Later, additional pressure was exerted for two days. The committee complied by announcing two days—the first and the last days of the conference. One would have to sit through a whole week of Norwegian to attend the second day of English.

In more recent years during the visit to a Spanish speaking congregation, I was approached by the young people with the complaint that "We want some services in English but the old people want everything in Spanish." It seemed to me history was repeating itself.

The Overseas Department recently received a letter from the Evangelical Free Church of Brazil asking for a copy of a constitution. On being asked the purpose of the request, the Department was told that the church had been established by the Free Evangelical Church of Germany, a sister denomination in the Federation of Free Evangelical Churches. The services in Brazil had always been in German but now the second generation demanded that the language be changed to the language of Brazil; namely, Portuguese. Again history repeats itself.

One of the more amusing stories is of a discussion that took place in a Swedish congregation. The Sunday services and business meetings had long been conducted in English but now the deacons had proposed that the prayer meeting also be led in English, though participants would be free to pray in whatever language they preferred. One of the older brethren protested, "It's all right to hold the Sunday service in English. After all, the American heathen need to hear the Gospel and be saved. I do not object to the business meetings being in English. After all, they are not very spiritual anyway. But to hold prayer meetings in English, that is something else again."

"May I ask the brother a question?" interrupted a younger man. "Do you mean that if I pray to God in English, He won't hear me?"

The first man was quiet for a moment while the members eagerly awaited his reply.

"Oh, He will hear you all right, but He ain't going to like it very much!"

On the denominational level, both the Swedish and Norwegian-Danish associations had to adjust to changing times. The conferences converted from the Scandinavian languages to English. The Norwegians made the change in 1933 and the Swedes in 1934. It was during that time that the names of the denominations were officially changed to English. This embodied the requirement that the reports and minutes be recorded in English and that both moderators and secretaries be bilingual in the first few years after the change. This also affected the official periodicals. The publication of the *Chicago Bladet* (Swedish) was terminated in 1952 and the *Evangelisten* (Norwegian) in 1955.

There was an important by-product to the shift in languages and the publication of papers in English—the *Evangelical Beacon* in 1931 and the *Evangelist* in 1927. Both denominations had published papers in English earlier. In due course the papers made a major contribution to the merger of the two denominations. With the language barriers removed, the constituency of both began to know and understand one another. A merger could not have been even considered until both spoke the same language.

C. T. Dyrnes, the pastor of the Salem Church in Chicago, revealed his vision when he wrote in 1921:

> We shall soon face the change of language. We are looking for the coming of the Lord, but must prepare for the change of language if the Lord should tarry. Either we cooperate with other groups of like faith and principles or we shall be swallowed up by the large denominations and what we have worked so hard to build up will be no more. We can now begin to cooperate in our home missions program, our foreign missions, and the work of the school without difficulty. In the school we can use different languages in certain subjects and cooperate where English is now used. The day will soon come when English will be used in all subjects and we might as well prepare for it now.[5]

David Nyvall, the first president of North Park College and prior to that a teacher in the Swedish Department of the Chicago Theological Seminary, who had expressed his alarm that some of the younger members of the church could not even understand a Swedish sermon, wrote three years later (1899):

> It will not be long before we reach the transition from Swedish to English. We are already beginning to notice that the younger generation prefers English. We have already virtually two mother tongues. We need pastors who, in their training among us have become one with us inwardly, one

with us in our faith and conviction regarding personal spiritual life and church polity, pastors who are able in English to transmit to succeeding generations this precious heritage of principle.[6]

An interesting statement written from Kansas in 1908 contains a mixture of nostalgia, vision and commitment to the higher principles.

Learning Swedish by our children constitutes the most important preparation for carrying on evangelical work in our mother tongue—the beautiful Swedish. Nevertheless, God's Word is not bound. If the Gospel must be spoken in coming generations in English, then so be it, if only God be allowed to speak.[7]

The Evangelical Free Church of America is now in the process of completing a full cycle and is back where congregations are once more bilingual. Had my generation been told that going through the difficult days of transition would prepare us for identical days one and two generations later, it would have scoffed. Consider what has happened. There are now congregations with services in French and English; Spanish and English; Chinese and English; Vietnamese, Japanese and English; and German and English. These are now going through a transition phase. Fortunately, there is counsel available, backed by a century of experience. May today's stumbles be fewer in the march to maturity.

FOOTNOTES—CHAPTER I

1. Montgomery, Marcus W., *A Word From The Holy Spirit in Sweden and Norway*, New York, American Home Missions Society, 1884, p.83.
2. In more recent years, a congregation still strongly Norwegian had a basketball team playing in a local church league. It consistently came out a champion not only because the members were good players but they could give directions to the teammates in Norwegian much to the frustration of the opponents who did not understand.
3. Olsson, Karl, *By One Spirit*, Covenant Press, Chicago, Ill. 1962, p. 486, 487.
4. *Covenant Yearbook*, 1912, p. 39-40.
5. *Evangelisten*, March 9, 1921.
6. *Covenant Yearbook*, 1896, p. 105.
7. Ibid., 1908, p. 42.

Chapter II
LIFE STYLES

The term "life style" was popularized by an Austrian psychologist in a book entitled *The Science of Living and Pattern of Life!* It was first applied to abnormal patterns of living; such as homosexuality, lesbianism and cohabitation without formal marriage.[1] It is now used to describe any pattern of living; even the norm, though a timely definition of the normal style is increasingly elusive. What was once rejected as abnormal is now acceptable in our society, while the old norms are ridiculed as out-of-date. The term "life style" in this chapter is applied simply to one's manner of living.

Sitting at a lunch counter in the Greater Cincinnati Airport, I was approached by a gentleman who asked if I was the president of The Evangelical Free Church of America. Upon an affirmative reply he asked, "Are your congregations believers' churches and are they pietistic?" He knew the terminology. Most members will answer a ready "yes" to the first part of the question while not even knowing the meaning of the second. For one who understands the meaning of pietism, an affirmative answer would be promptly forthcoming. One dictionary describes pietism as "Piety or godliness; devotion as distinguished from insistence on religious creeds or forms." It holds to a soundness of Christian doctrine which reveals itself in soundness of deportment. It insists that an inner faith must express itself outwardly, that conversion results in a new life moved by a new dynamic, that repentance involves not just a confession and deep sorrow for sin but a forsaking of sin as well. As one puts it, "If confession of sin is not reflected in the reformation of life, it is simply a sentimental and verbal experience."[2] Or, as another expresses it, "A Christian is not a man who feels repentant on Sunday for what he did on Saturday and is going to do again on Monday."[3] Pietism demands that the life square with the profession.

A pietist then is one who is convinced that a believer is not to be conformed to this world; but to be transformed by the renewing of his mind that he may prove what is the good, acceptable and perfect will of God (Romans 12:2). There is a separation, not isolation, *from* the world *to* Christ. The pietist believes that, though he has been set free from the law, there is a negative dimension to the Christian life arising out of a positive commitment to Jesus as Lord. After all, does not all of life involve certain restrictions? "There will always be negative aspects to any affirmation of life. It is impossible to go north without 'negotiating' the tendency to go south. One cannot have X without a surrender of much that is not X. One cannot walk the easy path of dalliance and at the same time reap the firm fruits of stern concentration. There must be a stripping off of everything superfluous if you intend to venture the highest peaks and you can arrive only after sincere discipline."[4]

Yes, the membership of the Evangelical Free Churches is composed of believers only and they are pietistic. The Golden Jubilee book of the Swedish Evangelical Free Church of America makes this plain:

> Great emphasis was put on a personal and conscious experience of the saving grace of God in the believer, which experience should be clearly manifested in the believer's life. "By their fruits ye shall know them" was the key slogan. Life became, therefore, simple enough. The eternal verities were near and tangible, though in reality they lie beyond sense and time. An uncompromising faith in God and a childlike trust in

His promises brought them near. Christianity was something real. It was more than a system of philosophy; it was a living and vital force.[5]

To fully understand and appreciate Pietism, one needs to go back into church history to the time that the concept was introduced. The church of Luther had become a creed-bound and sacramental institution. In that climate Pietism became for awhile a powerful and effective, though divisive movement on the continent of Europe and in Scandinavia. One of the factors was a return to the belief that Christianity is a way of life as well as a system of doctrine. The founders rediscovered the New Testament truth that Christian doctrine had to be implemented by a Christlike life.

The movement was started in Germany by Philip Jacob Spener (1635-1705). He came upon the scene when Lutheranism in his country as well as in Scandinavia was nothing more than a dead orthodoxy. Christianity had become a matter of making a mental assent to the creeds of the church. It involved the minimum requirement of attending the church or being brought at least four times in a life span for baptism, confirmation, marriage and burial. Spener, sensing the depth to which Luther's reformation had fallen, began a renewal by bringing people to his home for Bible study, prayer and a discussion of the previous Sunday's sermon. The classes became known as the *Collegia Pietatis* from which comes the name Pietist. It was given to Spener's followers in ridicule as was the name Christian at Antioch centuries earlier and Methodists later. Spener put his thoughts in writing by authoring a booklet, *"Pia Desideria"* (Hearts and Pious Desires) which set down six means of renewing the life of the Christian:

1. Meeting in groups to study the Bible. The text for the day used by the priest as a basis for his sermons was not enough. It was necessary to hold meetings where the entire Word of God could be studied. (The Readers Movement in Scan-

dinavia two centuries later revived this philosophy.)

2. Putting into practice the priesthood of all believers. The members as well as the priests are responsible for the spiritual life of the church.

3. A practical application of Christianity to the daily life.

4. A sympathetic and brotherly attitude in all religious controversies. This called for a limitation of doctrinal polemics. The renewal of the spiritual life was a better safeguard of orthodoxy than theological debates.

5. A reorganization of theological training in the universities with an insistence on conversion and emphasis on practical piety.

6. Simplicity and directness in preaching including the implanting of Christianity in the new and inner man, the soul of which is faith and its effects the fruits of life.

The book caused a storm of opposition from the clergy but the ideas caught on, nevertheless. The renewal was accompanied by a new interest in missionary activity, even to members of the Jewish community. "Spener laid emphasis on the personal and spiritual life rather than merely on an intellectual acceptance of the doctrines of the church. In his preaching he denounced dancing, theater going, card playing, novel reading, elegant and gay clothing, light conversation and immoderate eating and drinking."[6]

There was a long journey from the days of Spener to the time of the Free Church pioneers. Though Pietism had reached the State Churches, resulting in an attempt, to a limited degree, to place a new emphasis on Christian living, by 1880 it was pretty much of a spent force within the Church. The principles, however, were picked up by the pioneers in the dissenter or Free Church movements.

In the book, *The Significance of Silence*, I quoted from letters written by Paul Peter Waldenstrom (1838-1917), the

Swedish theologian and one of the founders of the Free Mission Society in his country. He was a well educated, scholarly, ordained minister of the State Church until he withdrew to participate in the beginning of the formation of the dissenter movement. Although his dispute with the church was primarily over the doctrine of the atonement, he was also the eye of the storm over communion—to whom—by whom—and where it should be served. His letter written in October of 1876 reveals the moral conditions of the people and how far they had drifted from the principles of Pietism:

> How long shall we do without this means of grace? Was it not instituted for us? Yes, is it not necessary for us? Was it not the intent of the Lord that we should often celebrate the remembrance of His death?
>
> Many times when I have been faced with this situation the following question has come to mind: On the one hand, I see men—both priests and laymen—drink, play cards, dance, joke, and curse but there is no one who calls them separatists. On the other hand, I see a little flock gathered in all simplicity to confess their sins, to read God's Word and to break bread together and we call these separatists. What kind of a church is it then from which one considers separating if one wishes to follow Christ and the example of the apostles; but from which one does not consider separating if one frequents a public house (prostitution), lives in drunkenness, lewdness, cursing and other evils? Can it actually be the Church of Christ, yes, can it be the Lutheran Church which does not see any separatism therein when men live in open ungodliness; but, on the other hand, call it separatism when believers wish to live according to the Gospel of Christ? No, and again No! As little as it is separatism when Christians sever themselves from all other wrong doing; just as little do I believe one can call it separatism if some Christians sever themselves from the communion service where unworthy participation undoubtedly prevails.[7]

Denied the use of the Cathedral for a communion service for believers only, though he had the authority to do so as a duly recognized priest of the church, Waldenstrom went to the Mission House in defiance of the church law—a crime for which he was subsequently found guilty and ordered to pay a fine of 40 crowns. In a letter to a secular newspaper in Gothenburg, which revealed again his appraisal of the moral condition of Sweden at that time, he wrote:

> For a certainty it was with strange emotions that several hundred of us gathered in the Mission Chapel after being barred from the churches which time after time had been permitted to be used for concerts and similar affairs. We had requested permission to arrange for holding a communion service in the church which would be valid in accordance with the laws of the church; but this we were denied, so now we were assembled in the Mission Chapel fully aware that the Cathedral hierarchy would never waste any time in making an issue of it. We would never have had to fear any reprisal had we gathered about a glass of punch and engaged in dancing or card playing besides jesting and cursing; but now—driven out from the church—meeting together in a chapel to break bread in the name of Jesus and to praise His name, we could have no doubt about what the outcome would be. Oh, it really seemed very odd that in a protestant country which boasts of its evangelical stance and religious freedom one should expect such treatment.[8]

Similar conditions existed in Norway and Denmark. In his autobiography, written in Danish, Nils C. Carlsen describes the life style of his childhood community in Denmark:

> The amount of godliness in the home of my parents and grandparents was no different than in others of my community. People were baptized, confirmed, served the Lord's Supper (at the most once a year). When Christmas arrived someone had to bring the annual compulsory offerings to the church, one for the priest and one for the school teacher. Many families persuaded someone else to bring it so they wouldn't have to attend church themselves. If one failed to pay, a representative would call demanding payment.

> We had neither a Bible nor a book of sermons in the house. Even though I had travelled across the entire country I had never seen a Bible in any home until I came to America and

by then I was 25 years of age. No one in my entire family had such a book until I bought one 12 years later as a gift to my mother who was then close to seventy.

We did own a hymnal (salme bog) from which was read some verses a couple of times a year. On Christmas Eve, after completing the meal and before we began a game of cards and drinking whiskey and rum, someone read a Christmas hymn.

I never saw or heard anyone praying to God, either among young or old. All drank. Yet the members of my family were looked upon as honorable people. Children were served whiskey before 24 hours old. The first word many of them learned was an oath and so called upon the name of the devil. Most of the boys learned how to use tobacco before they started school and I was one of them.

None of our school teachers, as far as I know, were converted. At least this was true in the three schools I attended. Some may have held to higher moral standards than others but I never saw a teacher pray to God or read from the Bible. (Teachers were approved by the State Church and were supposed to be qualified to teach the religion of the State. ATO)

Most of them drank until they were drunk, played cards, cursed and were guilty of many immoralities which naturally followed the above mentioned sins.[9]

The situation was no different in Norway. One of the leaders in the awakening which preceded the Readers' Revival and Free Church movement by almost a century was Hans Nielsen Hauge (1771-1824). Haugianism had its roots in Pietism as it came out of Germany. His preaching called for not only a change of heart but of life style. "He translated deep religious conviction into patriotism, high morals, independent thinking, economic initiative and the removal of old class barriers."[10]

The fact that he did infers that they were missing in Norwegian society at that time. "It is not very easy to assess the spiritual conditions of those times," wrote a Lutheran historian, "but from what is known of the widespread inadequacy of both orthodoxy and rationalism, it was appropriate that the Hauge revival did lay great stress on a living faith."[10] Hauge directed much of his preaching against the clergy, although towards the end of his life he exhorted his followers to remain loyal to the State Church. In one of his attacks the interpretation of the passage from the book of Revelation may differ from the interpretation by evangelical scholars today. The matter of interest in this discussion is his judgment on the leaders of the church in his time and not his exegesis:

> The worldly claim that each one should remain in that state where he is called, after Paul's word in I Corinthians 7:20, and the pastors say they are installed by God and the king to preach God's word. But if they were installed by God, He would have taught them (John 6); they would have received freely and given freely (Matthew 10:8); they would have preached in season and out of season, admonished and exhorted; yes, if they had the mind of Christ, then they would sorrow night and day over wickedness. But now they are the great whore who sits on the many waters (Revelation 17:1), . . . They sit upon the scarlet colored beast, full of names of blasphemy, which has seven heads and ten horns (v. 3), which beast is the ungodly authorities, and the seven heads are the seven prayers in the Lord's Prayer which they pray with the mouth in such a manner that their hearts become hard as mountains inasmuch as they commit sins against each petition, and make it a common practice.[11]

It is out of this moral climate that the immigrants came to America. Here they found matters even worse. The circumstances are well described in the anniversary book:

> Infidelity and gross ungodliness were triumphant in many sections of the country. Religion seemed in these places to have gone to seed. As a matter of fact it was on the point of extinction. Something extraordinary was necessary to arrest the attention of the people, who were ready to conclude that Christianity was a delusion.[12]

Immigrants who had not been touched by the revivals in the homeland gravitated to the same low moral standards.

The report prepared for Marcus Montgomery prior to his going to Scandinavia as recorded in the previous chapter included reference to the moral condition among the immigrants:

> In vices they are also much like Americans. Intemperance is sometimes said to be their national besetting sin. Like other Northern nations, they have a partiality for the stronger liquors as against wines and beer; and yet too many of them accept anything that will intoxicate. As regards profanity, gambling, and licentiousness, they are much in need of the converting power of the Gospel.[13]

The revivals changed this conclusion. The converts, with the help of the Holy Spirit and a study of the Scriptures, were transformed into a new life style. They discovered that the Christian life involved negatives but always with accompanying positives. The letter of Paul to the Ephesians was only one of the many passages which convinced them of the importance of being converted to a new way of living:

> If so be that ye have heard him, and have been taught by him, as the truth is in Jesus:
>
> That ye put off concerning the former conversation the old man, which is corrupt according to the deceitful lusts;
>
> And be renewed in the spirit of your mind; And that ye put on the new man, which after God is created in righteousness and true holiness.
>
> Wherefore putting away lying, speak every man truth with his neighbor: for we are members one of another.
>
> Be ye angry, and sin not: let not the sun go down upon your wrath: Neither give place to the devil.
>
> Let him that stole steal no more: but rather let him labour, working with his hands the thing which is good, that he may have to give to him that needeth.

Let no corrupt communication proceed out of your mouth, but that which is good to the use of edifying, that it may minister grace unto the hearers.

And grieve not the holy spirit of God, whereby ye are sealed unto the day of redemption.

Let all bitterness, and wrath, and anger, and clamor, and evil speaking, be put away from you, with all malice:

And be ye kind one to another, tenderhearted, forgiving one another, even as God for Christ's sake hath forgiven you (Ephesians 4:21-32).

Judging by the statements from the pens of Waldenstrom and Carlsen, the cardinal sins of the old life were drinking of alcoholic beverages, using tobacco, playing cards, dancing and the desecration of the Sabbath. These were the first sins of the old life to be abandoned. Generally, this continues to be the priority.

The conference at Boone, Iowa, in 1884, though assembled to study the structure of the church and how the new, young congregations could work together to carry out the Lord's instructions in the Great Commission, also considered the matter of life style. The statements on the church have been well publicized but paragraph five of the document is not so well known:

As members of God's commonwealth in this land, we wish, as did Israel of old, prosperity to the land wherein we dwell, and pledge ourselves to seek its best. To that end we do hereby oppose all lasciviousness and crime, knowing that sin is the ruin of any nation. Especially do we express our abhorrence of such barbaric and degenerating practices as drunkenness and polygamy, which practices cause great hindrance to the furtherance of the Gospel and the salvation of people. On the other hand, we do pledge ourselves to further and cooperate in every effort put forth to quell such iniquities in every honorable purpose and plan. We are also convinced, especially in regard to combating the liquor evil, that its presentation as a special feature without associating it with other social or political questions, will find the best support in the community, state, and nation, such as a total prohibition of the manufacture, sale and use of intoxicants. This goal we earnestly pray God soon may grant us in His mercy.[14]

The reference to polygamy introduced a sin not listed in the statements by leaders in Scandinavia. This is another example of new life styles found by the immigrants. Polygamy was practiced by the Mormons. The leaders at the Boone conference were very sensitive to this because of the missionary activity in Utah by some in attendance.

Almost a century later (1979) the conference adopted the following as one of its resolutions:

That as the Lord tarries we give ourselves to a Godly life-style in contrast to the self satisfying society, and that we renew our support to the family unit and morality that is taught in the Word of God.

That we give ourselves to holy, righteous living setting an example to our nation and being available and usable to the Holy Spirit in His ministry of glorifying Jesus Christ.

In seeking a godly life the founders and the next generation faced two dangers. Incidentally, they are two dangers ever with us.

The first was the danger of *reductionism;* that is, reducing the Christian life to a narrow list of taboos and demanding that all, in every culture and generation, follow the same blueprint. This robbed the first generation born in America of much that rightly was a part of liberty in Christ, individualism, and spontaneity. The local membership often became like a box of matches—all alike and burning for a brief time—rather than like candles, some tall, some short, some narrow and some wide, but all shining brightly according to their capacity.

It is a fact of history that the Pietistic movement sometimes led to legalism and even fanaticism as far as a concept of total Christian behavior is concerned.

The second danger was that of *confusing the Christian life style with cultural conformity*. This seemed to work both ways. On one hand practices were considered sinful simply because they had not been a part of the life style in the old country. On the other, and just the opposite, practices were acceptable because "everyone was doing it."

The immigrants also found extremes which were alien to them. There were sects in America, most of which had patterns of behavior peculiar to them. There were, for example, the hook and eye people whose garments were held together by hooks rather buttons since the use of the latter was considered sinful. There was a sect recognized by the absence of the necktie. Following the invention of the automobile there have been those who, even to this day, refuse to change from horse and buggy to car. The women wear their traditional bonnets while the men use the widely brimmed black hats. The Diamond Jubilee Story reveals that the pioneers were not beyond similar negatives. Some of them "advocated a kind of 'separation' that went to extremes in the matter of dress, such as a refusal to wear jewelry (even a wedding ring), to use a necktie, to curl the hair, wear a feather in the hat, etc. Men of intelligence and mature judgment, like Princell, did their best to warn people against such extremes . . . " As for Princell, a later story in this chapter reveals that he was not exactly invulnerable to similar ideas.[15]

Such extremes did not end with the first decade. They had even more trouble with the changing life styles as time went on. Often what was merely a shift in current cultural habits were mistaken for signs of apostasy.

The following story, though not directly related to religious life styles, might well have been.

As recently as ten years ago at a high school commencement, a young graduate was not permitted to walk across the stage to receive his diploma. It was handed to him as he stood down on the main floor. This, even though he had been a top student in the class, was a leader in student activities, had bridged the generation gap and got along well with his peers. What was wrong? He wore a beard in defiance of school rules. He claimed it wasn't much of a beard but he felt it did make him look like Abraham Lincoln, the greatest of American presidents.

The fiftieth anniversary book of the Swedish Evangelical Free Church shows pictures of twenty of its most illustrious pioneers. Twelve have beards, seven mustaches and only one was clean shaven. He was considered one of the more radical of the pioneers. Could it be he showed his defiance of tradition in being clean shaven? It was said in those days that when the younger men shaved off their beards mothers wept because their sons appeared effeminate!

There was a narrow line between what was under the law and what was under grace. Christian responsibility under grace was sometimes interpreted according to background, geographic location or the misreading of the Word. The matter of works before or after salvation was often misplaced and became so confusing that some abandoned works altogether.

One member of a congregation I served was so afraid of confusing law with grace that whenever I spoke on some aspect of Christian responsibility, such as stewardship, separation, etc., he would comment on leaving the service at its close, "Pastor, you preached the law today." But when the message dealt with liberty in Christ, Christian joy, heaven, etc., the appraisal would be, "Pastor, you were in on grace today."

In reducing life to a narrow list of taboos, there developed a constant feeling of guilt which became the breeding ground for inhibitions, frustrations, anxiety and hostility; whereas antinomianism, in the extreme, led to licentiousness. Fortunately, most of the pioneers found the balance between works and faith, freedom in Christ and commitment to Christ, separation and isolationism, culture and conformity. They also were able to accept a self-imposed restraint on behavior. They found some things may have been lawful but not always expedient (I Cor. 6:12; 10:23). They were concerned about the conversion of fellow immigrants and the spiritual growth of the new converts. These were facing the same two dangers they had met in their early Christian experience.

Let us not therefore judge one another any more: but judge this rather, that no man put a stumblingblock or an occasion to fall in his brother's way.

I know, and am persuaded by the Lord Jesus, that there is nothing unclean of itself: but to him that esteemeth any thing to be unclean, to him it is unclean.

But if thy brother be grieved with thy meat, now walkest thou not charitably. Destroy not him with thy meat, for whom Christ died.

Let not then your good be evil spoken of:

For the kingdom of God is not meat and drink; but righteousness, and peace, and joy in the Holy Ghost.

For he that in these things serveth Christ is acceptable to God, and approved of men.

Let us therefore follow after the things which make for peace, and things wherewith one may edify another.

For meat destroy not the work of God. All things indeed are pure; but it is evil for that man who eateth with offence.

It is good neither to eat flesh, nor to drink wine, nor any thing whereby thy brother stumbleth, or is offended, or is made weak (Romans 14:13-21).

Concern for a weaker brother was also in danger of being carried to the extreme. Some weaker brothers could use it to their advantage while some more experienced believers became slaves to public opinion. While I was in my first pastorate, golf started to become a popular pastime and I began to play the game. One of my deacons confronted me one Sunday morning following the service in the presence of others with the following, "Pastor, I hear you have taken up the game of golf." In my reply to the affirmative, he continued, "Don't you know that it is sin?" I answered that I had not seen it as such. He then said, "Well, if you don't think it is, you should at least stop lest you offend your weaker brother." I asked if he might tell me who had been offended so that I could explain the game. His answer was brief. "Me!"

One development in the early days was that while attacking preachers and American denominations for taking away portions of the Scripture (creation, Jonah and the whale, etc.) they themselves were guilty of adding prohibitions to the Word that were not even suggested in it. But as they grew in grace and knowledge they moved on to maturity also in the area of life style, though there were stumbles along the way.

The practice of reductionism drove prospects for conversions away. Christianity was made unattractive. The following are a few examples of inconsistencies—some in the area of legalism and others in antinomianism —which illustrate both extremes. We will begin with the sins condemned at the beginning of the chapter and conclude with some where culture and correct Christian behavior were sometimes confused.

The question of liquor or, as the Scandinavians were prone to call it, *strong drink,* was not one of controversy. I do not recall a single sermon from childhood days against the use of intoxicating beverages, though I heard many stories about men and women who were delivered from their use upon conversion. In fact, in some places one who died a drunkard was buried just outside the fence of the church cemetery. This was true in one church I served. Silence on the subject indicated that warnings were not needed. The early members simply did not drink and they had a deep abhorrence of the practice. Temperance movements in Scandinavia coincided with the revivals. In

America it was not unusual to find church members active in the former Anti-Saloon League and supporters of the prohibition amendment in spite of a reluctance to get involved in politics.

Some older congregations wrote rules for behavior into their by-laws which were primarily negative. Endeavoring to catalogue sins created interesting consequences. The Bible does present principles as a guide for conduct but it cannot, because of the time in which it was written, always be specific. Since it is the Book of the ages for men, women and children of all languages and cultures, it is fortunate that this is case. This is part of what makes this ancient Book so contemporary.

In one community a small group of believers had just moved from one city where they had been members of an Evangelical Free Church. In listing taboos for the by-laws, in the process of organizing a new congregation, they added the following postscript, "We are against everything the _____ church (the former congregation) is against and we are against strong drink, too." It seems in making a list of the sins to which they had objected, that church had inadvertently omitted any reference to intoxicating beverages.

One congregation in considering a new constitution went through a great deal of heated discussion as to whether or not it should accept a specific code of conduct or a covenant of understanding. The former was carried over from the earliest days since this was one of the original congregations, while the latter laid down principles rather than a list of do's and don'ts. One decried the suggestion that prohibitions not be included, accusing the advocates of permissiveness and compromise. Finally, a medical doctor, never known for much talking at business meetings, arose and said, "I see you want to go on record as being opposed to liquor and tobacco but favoring the use of narcotics, which in my profession I find to be one of the most destructive sins of all." The members were stunned, silenced and appalled at the very thought but saw the physician's point. The question was called for since the debate had ended and the second suggestion was adopted which read as follows and does to this day:

> The fundamental principles of this church are based upon the Word of God. Therefore every member of the church is expected to live according to its teachings and avoid and refrain from that which is destructive to the Christian life and dishonorable to God. Every member is earnestly admonished to refrain from slander and evil speaking of one another; to pray constantly for the Church, its members, and its ministry; to materially support the Church according to ability and necessity; to attend the services as far as possible; and to live a holy and godly life in the midst of a crooked and perverse generation.

In preparation for this chapter I have talked to several of my generation regarding dancing and playing cards, mentioned repeatedly in the beginning. A surprising majority have difficulty identifying the cards in a pack and confess to not knowing one dance step from another.

The fear of desecrating the Sabbath went so deep that one wondered if boys and girls were made to glorify Sunday or if Sunday was started for the pleasure of the children. On the other hand, the extremes to which even believers have gone in the other direction once permissiveness became the order of the day makes one, in retrospect, think that maybe the restrictions in my childhood were not as bad as they seemed then.

Sunday was the day for church—all day for church! First, there was Sunday School followed by a ten minute break and then the morning service in Norwegian lasting one and a half hours, at least. To me, as to most children, every sermon was too long. The morning worship over, we would return to our homes for dinner, read the Sunday School papers and have a brief rest. In the late afternoon we returned to the church for the youth meeting, also in Norwegian. The best part of the day came when refreshments were served following that service. It was a wonderful time for the young immigrants since it was the hour when they could exchange news from the villages across the sea and even arrange for a date or two. The evening service was a repetition of the morning session with one exception, for this was a time of revival and the altar call brought many forward for the aftermeeting which usually lasted longer than the service itself. I sat in the front pew at most services and fell asleep on the cushioned pews shortly after the evening service began, only to be partly awakened to be moved back several rows to make room for those seeking salvation and those praying with and for them. Many reading this account will do so with a sense of nostalgia. One result was that Sunday was made something special and remains so to this day.

Many sermons were preached against "coffin nails" and the "weed." The use of tobacco was a sin and a violation of the Scriptures. I listened in vain for the specific chapter and verse. It took medical science to spell out the danger by exposing the use of tobacco as a cause of cancer and emphysema resulting in a shortening of the life span. This led to a federal law requiring a warning on each package of cigarettes. There are also smoking and non-smoking sections on commercial airplanes as well as separate sections and even complete railroad cars for smokers and non-smokers. Some states have passed laws calling for designated no smoking sections in public buildings. In spite of the lack of scientific data in the early days, few Free Church members practiced the use of tobacco in any form. In fact, if one lit up a smoke on leaving the church we would have concluded that the smoker was a visitor. There was a danger, however, that non-smoking, like other negatives, would come to be considered an evidence of being a true Christian. I am reminded of a friend who, in addressing the students at the college where he was president, illustrated this danger by saying, "If I ask some of you whether or not you are a Christian many would answer, 'Yes, I am.' If I should go further and ask what evidence can you produce to show that you are, you would answer, 'I refuse to bear arms.' " The denomination of that college is one of the evangelical, pacifist bodies. I told him that some of our people would reply, "Well, I don't smoke and I don't drink."

The question of whether or not the use of tobacco was sin was debated at mission conferences. One lady related that in her youth she had heard someone publicly accuse Princell of smoking in secret and condemned him for it. Just then there was a noise in the balcony as the professor lifted his massive frame from a pew on which he had been lying. Rising to his full height with booming voice he responded, "Yes, and the professor also prays in secret." The crowd was shocked to see him. With that comment he lay down to sleep some more. The discussion ended leaving some not exactly sure of the relationship between smoking in secret and praying in secret.

E. A. Halleen, with his unique gift of expression, wrote in his autobiography of a meeting where the question of tobacco was being discussed.

Whether belonging to one class or the other, as a rule our brethren were straight shooters, and hidebound individualists to the Nth degree. They spoke right from the shoulder. A mere glance at the topics that would come up for discussion at ministerial and annual meetings will convince one of that. And always there would be a practical application made openly and publicly. At the time the policy of *Chicago Bladet*, then a privately owned publication, was contrary to the wishes of some, the question was discussed at an annual meeting, "Can a newspaper man ever hope to get to heaven?" The consensus was: he may hope to get there but it is unlikely that he will succeed. At another annual meeting it was noised about that a few of the clergy were indulgers of the "weed." A discussion ensued and some fiery anathemas hurled against the culprits. A well-known and bitter opponent to the usage led the discussion. At the close he called on the oldest and sweetest dispositioned among us to close with prayer. Being small of stature, the brother called upon usually wore a high silk hat. This he carried with him to the platform. As he knelt to pray he first spread a red handkerchief on the platform, placed the hat thereon and folded his hands on the hat and in beautiful Swedish and with an intimacy that indicted a lifelong friendship, he began, "My Father, I thank You for graciously conceding to me that which my brethren so violently condemn."

* * * * * *

It is needless to say, our brother scored a victory. The game was over. The moral issue involved was naturally not settled, but we were. And we deserved it—the acrid subject had been acridly discussed. I cannot recall that this question has been submitted for open discussion since the aforementioned meeting. In later years there have been so many major questions pertaining to the work that demanded attention that we have had no time for idle discussions.

That a discussion "may be started on any point at any distance from that point" was one of the witty propositions laid down in Lewis Carrol's *Improved Euclid*. The statement was so obvious that it needed no proof. It is equally obvious, as someone has remarked, "that a discussion on any point might end at any distance from that point—if only it will end and be done with." But that seldom happens. Between the beginning and ending there usually occur many words and useless controversy. That and hurt feelings.[16]

Today, Free Church people are still among the non-smokers. At the 1980 General Conference with up to 2,500 people in attendance, there were literally no cigarette butts or cigar stubs outside the exits. The only change is the motivation. Men and women do not abstain to prove their Christian faith or to comply with some code of conduct in the church. The body is the temple of the Holy Spirit and they do not wish to desecrate it.

As time went on the early believers, as some even do today, began to add to the taboos such practices as were unknown when they first arrived in America.

There were changes in dress and hair styles. Sermons were preached against the sin of "bobbed hair" among women and their use of cosmetics. Some choir members had to leave the choir once they "compromised" and succumbed to the temptation to cut their hair short. Sermons were invariably directed only at women. It was really a form of male chauvinism. As an illustration of the extremes to which some went there is a story from an earlier period when the attack was on the style of rolling the hair into a knot on the top of the head. In addition to the passage on braided hair or platted hair, one evangelist went so far as to announce as his subject "Top Knot Come Down." He based it on a strange misuse of Matthew 24:17: "Let him that is on the house *top not* come down."

Nothing was said to the men about their changing hair styles or use of cosmetics. When women's skirts first became shorter a new sermon topic was added to the arsenal. When slacks for women became popular there was an even louder protest. Some even condemned short sleeved dresses. Nothing was ever said about the fact that in New Testament time, and even today, men in the Middle East wore skirts.

I attended my first youth conference while still in my early teens. The services were held in a large tent. The ground inside was covered with gravel—really chips from a quarry and had sharp corners. One of the Free Church evangelists blasted the young ladies for not kneeling during the altar call, accusing them of being more concerned about runs in their silk stockings than about sinners running from God. I looked around and saw that the men were not kneeling either but nothing was said to them.

Mrs. Esther Wedell told me years ago of an unforgettable experience. In preparation for attendance at a mission meeting in Omaha, she purchased a new hat with a feather added for decoration. When Princell saw it he condemned the feather as denoting worldliness. She was so embarrassed that she went to the alley in back of the church, ripped off the feather and tossed it into a garbage can. Only then could she feel she had met the professor's standard of true spirituality.[17]

I recall only one charge made against men. It happened when men's styles shifted from high shoes to oxfords, and to compensate for the ankles being cold in winter, spats became popular. These were buttoned on the side with straps under the soles. It was also a time when men started to abandon hats. I heard L. J. Pedersen, president of the Minneapolis Free Church school, condemn both. He also condemned me personally, in the presence of others, for conforming to these "worldly practices." I wondered at that time if the fact that he still wore high shoes and was quite bald prompted him to consider the new life style carnal. He was a man of understanding in everything else.

Scriptures eventually won the victory even in the area of dress and hair styles. The Lord looked upon the heart. Inner beauty took priority. Modesty was becoming. However, the remnants of such attitudes still persist. They are not always dropped into the generation gap. I was informed not long ago that "our summer conferences are more spiritual than at any other camp. We don't allow the girls to wear slacks or shorts at any time." Actually, the rules are set up by the camp as an extension of the congregational system, but to equate such rules with spirituality is again confusing culture and Biblical principles.

Radio and television when first introduced were both looked upon with suspicion primarily because they were new. Being the son of progressive parents, I received a radio for Christmas. It consisted of a small black box, a large spool of copper wire, a crystal, a "cat's whisker" and one earphone. It was built by an exemplary member of the church who was an engineer. A deacon warned my father that he should know better than to permit Satan to enter into his son's life through a little black box. I thought that Satan entered the heart before there were black boxes and was not the radio made by a good member of the church who was also the leader of the string band?

Then came television. Grandparents would not enter the room where the set stood, especially when it was on. The believers were sincere in their caution. It must be noted to their credit that, though slow to accept new things, they did move on. Theirs was not so much a reaction against new things as a reverence for the Old Book.

The Christian church following the admonition to prove all things and hold fast to that which is good has taken advantage of radio, television and movies to further the cause of the Gospel of Jesus Christ. A surprising number of Evangelical Free Church congregations were among the first in America to broadcast services and other programs. One associate reaches by radio more people with one sermon than all the apostles together reached in a lifetime (40 million) and in more languages (45) than were heard on the Day of Pentecost.

It was reported in 1978 that 1300 radio stations, one out of every seven in America, was Christian owned and operated and reached a listening audience of 150 million people. Every seven days a new Christian owned radio station is established.[18]

As to television, Christian broadcasters are adding one new owned and operated station every thirty days.[19] Christian stations claim a viewing audience of thirteen million households or nearly 20 percent of the entire United States viewing public.[20] This does not take into account the Christian telecasts on commercial networks which as early as 1970 amounted to 500 million dollars in purchased air time.[21]

A report issued in March of 1981 stated that in an average week, 47 percent of the population of the United States tunes in to at least one religious program while only 42 percent attend church services. That's quite a change from the earlier days of broadcasting.

When it comes to films, what began as promoting missions has now become a major means of evangelism with large companies producing Christian films. But, like radio and television, movies had tough going in many Christian communities. Churches were even divided over whether or not to permit missionaries to show slides except in some of the more worldly minded homes. Movies appeared even before the question of slides was settled in some congregations. Three lads in one of the churches, whose father had passed away and whose mother was incapacitated, begged the mother for permission to go to church and view some missionary slides, a first for that church. They were simply enlarged pictures placed on a white sheet. She finally gave in but said to the oldest brother, "You may go but if the pictures start to wiggle you take your younger brothers and come right home."

In one of my pastorates the congregation was adamant against pictures at missionary conferences—still or moving. Then a favorite guest preacher returned from a tour of Norway where he had taken moving pictures. The leadership compromised by renting a hall for the showing, something never proposed for missionary films. It was also at a time when a Norwegian skating star turned actress was appearing in a picture featuring her skating. Some young people were severely condemned for going to a theater to see the film. However, when she came to the city in person to present the same routine accompanied by the same orchestra and other skaters, the critics did not hestitate to attend the show. This illustrates again the inconsistencies resulting from the reductionism introduced at the beginning of this chapter.

Finally, there was the matter of recreation such as bowling, playing pool, or Sunday baseball. Again we must note that these were new to the immigrants. There was little said in opposition to games brought from Europe. For example, horseshoe, tug-of-war, *siste par ut* (last couple out) were standard for a church picnic even on Sunday, though it all had to be sanctified with a religious service prior to game time. Before becoming too critical we should note that bowling was associated with liquor and pool with pool halls and saloons. Now we have church bowling leagues and pool tables in many Christian homes. Is that a compromise? It was the unknown that caused caution and the association that brought criticism.

We must not close the chapter with the discussion limited to the evidences of immaturity, carnality, etc. The title would be in error if the book dealt only with the stumbles while ignoring the growth. First, we will consider the charge in approach to wordly amusements and then some of the serious moral problems the Christian and the Church face today. In all cases we shall note that the danger of reductionism and confusing culture with what is right or wrong has been overcome by following the original premise of the Free Church movement, "Where stands it written?" All questions must be considered in the light of Biblical principles introduced centuries ago and long before certain life styles become the "in thing."

In 1952 Donald Larson, while a teacher at Trinity, the Evangelical Free Church school, wrote a tract, "Taboo or not Taboo" in which he outlined a series of tests young people might use in determining the answer to two questions—"What kind of amusements?—How much of the kind if at all?" He presented six test questions about the first and four on the second. The tract has been printed several times and is used among Free Church youth groups today. In trying to decide how to present the highlights, I have concluded that it might best be included in full.[22]

The pale blue Pacific would be a deep purple today if all the ink spilled on the subject of "worldly amusements" were to flow into the great body of water . . . and here is another contribution to the endeavor.

Maybe you're planning on a bit of recreation this weekend. You may indulge in a fast game of horseshoes, or a set of pingpong . . . or perhaps your inclinations run along Chinese Checker lines. If you're the intellectual type, you'll play a game of Scrabble (with an unabridged dictionary, of course). Maybe you have something more vigorous in mind—like bowling, or skating, or maybe swimming.

No matter what you have in mind, someone will raise a finger of caution or roll his eyeballs at you. If you live in the South, you can't do this, if you're from the North, that other thing is just out of the question. You're from the East end of a big city . . . over there you can't do this, but on the other side of town it's O.K.

Who's right? Who's wrong? When can I, and when can't I do this? What can I do that nobody will gripe about? How can a young Christian have any fun? These are perplexing questions. You've heard every one of them. You've heard the answers too . . . answers based on experience, on theories, on educated guesses, and even on nothing at all.

Let's try another answer—one from the Bible. But first a few fundamental facts: 1) Paul says in Romans that he believes nothing is evil in itself. 2) The matter of "questionable amusements" seems to vary with the geographical location. 3) The Bible mentions very clearly one standard of conduct, described in various ways:

> 1) "Sanctify yourselves therefore, and be ye holy: for I am the Lord your God."   Leviticus 20:7

> 2) "You have been bought, and at what a price! Therefore bring glory to God both in your body and your spirit, for they both belong to Him."
>   I Corinthians 6:20

> 3) "For the grace of God, which can save every man, has now become known, and it teaches us to have no more to do with godlessness or the desires of this world but to live, here and now, responsible, honourable and God-fearing lives."   Titus 2:11-12

WHAT KIND OF RECREATION?

The matter of recreation divides itself into two parts, one dealing with "what kind," the other with "how much". Here is a set of test questions with their scriptural answers. Check the correct answer in your own case.

1) Does this recreation harm me in any way—like physically? Yes____ No____ "Don't you realize that you yourselves are temples of God, and that God's Spirit lives in you? God will destroy anyone who defiles His temple, for His temples are holy—and that is exactly what you are!" I Corinthians 3:16-17.

2) Am I being so friendly with unbelievers that I'm losing my contact with fellow Christians by doing this? Yes____ No____ "Don't link up with unbelievers and try to work with them" II Corinthians 6:14.

3) Am I getting so wrapped up in this thing that I'm losing my self-control? Yes_____ No_____ "Watch and pray, all of you, that you may not have to face temptation. Your spirit is willing, but human nature is weak" Matthew 26:41.

4) Am I ignoring what effect my actions may have on others? Yes_____ No_____ "Treat men exactly as you would like them to treat you." Luke 6:31.

5) Am I promoting evil rather than good by my participation in this activity? Yes_____ No_____ "Anyone who is not with me is against me, and the man who does not gather with me is really scattering" Luke 11:23.

6) Am I pouring dollars and dimes down the drain, thus endangering my own or my family's welfare? Yes_____ No_____ "Tell those who are rich in this present world not to be contemptuous of others, and not to rest the weight of their confidence on the transitory power of wealth but on the living God, who generously gives us everything for our enjoyment. Tell them to do good, to be rich in kindly actions, to be ready to give to others and to sympathize with those in distress. Their security should be invested in the life to come, so that they may be sure of holding a share in the Life which is permanent" I Timothy 6:17-19.

HOW MUCH?

Now let's look at another set of questions and answers dealing with "how much" recreation.

1) Have I participated in this thing so much that my conscience is so insensitive that it does not bother me any more? Yes_____ No_____ "Yet if a man eats meat with an uneasy conscience about it, you may be sure he is wrong to do so. For his action does not spring from his faith, and when we act apart from our faith we sin" Romans 14:23.

2) Am I getting to the point where I have to rationalize about this activity? Yes_____ No_____ "Bodily fitness has a certain value, but spiritual fitness is essential" I Timothy 4:8.

3) Have I been spending so much energy on this thing that I don't have enough left to serve Christ? Yes_____ No_____ " . . . loving all the time what gives them pleasure instead of loving God. They will maintain a facade of 'religion,' but their conduct will deny its validity" II Timothy 3:4.

4) Am I losing interest in spiritual things after participating in this thing? Yes_____ No_____ "Live life, then, with a due

sense of responsibility, not as men who do not know the meaning and purpose of life but as those who do. Make the best use of your time, despite all the difficulties of these days" Ephesians 5:15.

5) And the solution to this problem would not be complete without a reference to Colossians 3:17:

"And whatever work you may have to do, do everything in the Name of the Lord Jesus, thanking God the Father through Him."

SO WHAT?

Maybe you had to answer "yes" to some of these questions. Your duty is to separate yourself from things which reduce your effectiveness for Christ, according to Scripture. You will be driving out elements of worldliness from your life if you are sincere about living for Christ.

But maybe you could honestly answer "no" to all these questions. Then you have found a constructive, pleasurable and relaxing diversion from the everyday grind . . . you have discovered that recreation is not the same as worldliness.

Recreation isn't evil in itself if you can do it and still answer "no" to those questions. This recreation can really be called Christian recreation. Even in your own area this recreation wouldn't be called questionable. Hence the Bible has become your *real standard* for recreation.

Paul says "Your personal convictions are a matter of faith between yourself and God, and you are happy if you have no qualms about what you allow yourself to eat" (Romans 14:22).

Sure there's a line which divides the church from the world . . . a line drawn by the Bible, not by you and me.

Don't erase that line, don't wink at it and don't cross it.

(Translations from *The Gospels* and *Letters to Young Churches* by J. P. Phillips.)[22]

Emphasis has been placed on what we have chosen to call practices considered by the pioneers to be cardinal sins—drinking, the use of tobacco, card playing, dancing and the desecration of the Sabbath. There are practices today not necessarily new in that most of them have existed as long as there have been human beings on the face of the earth, but new in their acceptability in today's society. Further, they were unmentionables in the Christian vocabulary whether in the pew or from the pulpit. Many people, until recently, have not even known the meaning of the terms. Among these are abortion, drug abuse, homosexuality, lesbianism, cohabitation without marriage, divorce and remarriage.

Has the church matured or has the old method of merely preaching against these practices continued? Do we simply add new negatives to the list without seeking solutions or providing help for persons involved or those searching for truth? Are opinions still being formed by those with the loudest voices and usually one issue proneness? There has been no compromise nor abandonment of the question, "Where stands it written?" Maturity has added another dimension—a continued study of the Scriptures plus opportunity and helps to a study of the problems.

In 1961 the annual conference decided to appoint a Committee on Social Concerns.

> The Board of Directors shall appoint annually a committee of five members to serve as the Committee on Social Concerns. As far as possible the membership shall be composed of (1) a rural church pastor, (2) a city church pastor, (3) an individual trained and working in the field of social science or sociology, (4) an individual who has some special practical experience on one or more phases of social activity, (5) one who though not having special training or experience is vitally interested in this field. It shall be the duty of this committee to keep the Evangelical Free Church of America informed as to such matters which should be of concern to evangelicals in the area of social action and shall use every possible means to alert the constituency to the needs.

The committee has studied, sometimes for two to three years, subjects of mutual concern to the people. Action has moved in two directions. First, the committee has prepared resolutions. In adopting these the denomination provides a consensus of opinion on the subjects named.

These cannot be forced on any member. In true congregational fashion, each individual makes his or her own decision, one that comes from within and is not imposed from some authority in the church. The basis for membership continues as stated in the doctrinal statement. It is a believers' church:

> That the true Church is composed of all such persons who through saving faith in Jesus Christ have been regenerated by the Holy Spirit and are united together in the body of Christ of which He is the Head (Article 8).

> That only those who are thus members of the true Church shall be eligible for membership in the local church (Article 9).

In this manner, the members can speak collectively. Second, the committee prepared sixteen to twenty page booklets which can be used as study guides for individuals and groups in aiding them not only to reach decisions but also to be able to present Biblical and intelligent answers to current questions. To date the conferences have adopted resolutions on the Family, Abortion and Homosexuality. The resolutions reveal that the two questions asked in the Cincinnati airport can still be answered in the affirmative.

RESOLUTION ON ABORTION, 1977

> We hold an unborn child to have the rights of a person from conception and that these rights may not be properly abrogated by law.

> We hold that it is the responsibility of parents to protect the rights of an unborn child and that abortion as commonly practiced today is not a legitimate means of handling unwanted, inconvenient or embarrassing pregnancies. We further hold that the rights of marriage should not be taken out of the context of marriage, but, even when they are, any resulting child is not to be viewed as having any less right to life and liberty from conception than any other child.

> We hold that the state should guarantee the rights of the unborn child as it would guarantee the rights of any of its citizens, but that where the state adopts a lesser morality it is

the duty of the Christian to adhere to and foster a higher morality.

We also hold that the eclectic morality currently upheld by the courts relative to abortion forbodes ill, not only for the defenseless, but also for the aged and the infirm, and represents an over-all trend which, if persisted in, will have repugnant consequences in the lives and consciences of every individual in our nation and in our national heritage and destiny.

Recognizing that the underlying social impetus to the abortion movement is the problem of unwanted children; we encourage our churches to take positive action in ministering to those situations where this problem of unwanted children exists. This could be done through counseling services, personal assistance to families where there is inability to provide for the means of children, and to become an agent of grace and support to the mother and her child.

RESOLUTION ON SINGLENESS, MARRIAGE AND THE FAMILY, 1977

In light of the million single adults in our society, we affirm singleness as a valid Biblical life style. I Cor. 7:8. Therefore, we encourage our churches to develop meaningful ministries to single persons and to see their essential role in the fellowship and ministry of the Body.

In light of the fact that one and one half million unmarried couples are living together in America, we affirm marriage as consistent with the Biblical norm.

In light of the million divorces occurring in the United States each year, we affirm the Biblical idea of marriage as being an indissoluble relationship and we regret the rising trend of divorce; and where it affects people within or without our churches we urge that our churches extend compassion and ministry to the affected.

In light of the widespread breakdown of the family in our society, we likewise affirm the importance of the family unit and its importance to the nurture and development of human life and the health of society.

Recognizing the pressures in our society that have contributed to the breakdown of marriage and the family, such as, the changing value systems, the high mobility of society and the impact of television; we urge the following:

1. The complexities of our modern industrial society has reduced the amount of time a family spends together. Therefore, it becomes increasingly important that the family compensate by carving out time to be together.

2. That the local church structure its program so as to allow sufficient time for family units to have time together.

3. That the local church help their families to develop meaningful family activities.

4. That parents take the initiative in relating more effectively to their children and to each other.

5. That parents use discretionary judgment not only in the selection of television programs, but also in the amount of time that television is in use in the home.

6. That parents give serious consideration to the implications of uprooting the famly for the sake of personal advancement.

7. That parents use Biblical family patterns and principles in the development of their family.

RESOLUTION ON HOMSEXUALITY, 1978

WHEREAS God in His Holy Word plainly condemns the practice of homosexuality as an abomination in His sight (Lev. 18:22), a degrading and unnatural passion (Rom. 1:26-27), one that brings grave consequences in this life, and a sin that if persisted in, will exclude one from the Kingdom of God (I Cor. 6:9-10), and

WHEREAS God desires that all repent and come to the knowledge of the truth and be saved, (II Pet. 3:9; I Tim. 2:4), and

WHEREAS through the Apostle Paul he testifies that homsexuals were among those who were washed, sanctified, and justified in the name of the Lord Jesus Christ (I Cor. 6:11),

BE IT THEREFORE RESOLVED

THAT neither individual Christians, nor ministers of the Word of God, nor congregations of the Lord Jesus Christ, may take away from or lessen God's prohibition of and warnings against the practice of homosexuality. Neither may they individually or collectively as responsible citizens in a free society, urge or concede that the state should give special protection or approval to this practice or promote it as a matter of personal taste, free choice, or "sexual orientation,"

THAT individual Christians, ministers and congregations, understanding that all human beings are sinners and that as Christian we have received God's mercy while helpless, ungodly and hostile to God (Rom. 3:23, 5:6, 10) must warn against homosexual practices as from the mouth of the Lord (Ezek. 3:17) and, at the same time proclaim forgiveness, cleansing, restitution and power for godly living for all who will repent and believe the Gospel (John 1:12, 3:16; Rom. 1:16; I Cor. 6:11; Phil. 2:13),

THAT individual Christians, ministers and congregations, compassionately and in love, should proclaim the Good News of forgiveness and the admonition to sin no more (John 8:11) to those once involved in homosexual practices, admitting them into fellowship after confession of faith and evidence of repentance, as with those who have sinned grievously in other ways (I Cor. 6:11).

Augustine wrote, "Love God and do as you please." Thus one pleases to so live and speak as to reflect his or her love for God. This is a good guide for all generations.

A study of God's Word eventually revealed to the founders, as it does to us today, a freedom from the law but also that this freedom isn't just a freedom from but a freedom to something. The Holy Spirit knew that, human nature being what it is, men would seek to rationalize reasons for a life style which is not under the burden of legalism. The Word, therefore, spells out bench marks for the Christian life style. The believer, once he reaches maturity, no longer looks upon life as a list of negations when he says a positive "yes" to the Lordship of Jesus Christ. This makes the yoke easy and the burden light (Matt. 11:30). He finds, as Paul writes in Ephesians 4, that as one puts off the old self, he puts on the new self which is in likeness of God created in righteousness and holiness of truth. As he lays aside lying, he goes on to speak truth to his neighbor. He may become angry but does not carry his anger beyond the setting of the sun. The one who stole hasn't just stopped stealing, but now works for a living with the proceeds shared with those in need. In dropping his unwholesome (rotten) language he goes on to use those words which are for "edification according to the need of the moment, that it may give grace to those who hear." The chapter then goes on to touch on matters which sometimes creep into that new life in its relationship to other believers. "Let all bitterness and wrath and anger and clamor and slander be put away from you with all malice." Even in these, the negative gives way to the positive, "And be ye kind to one another, tenderhearted, forgiving each other just as God in Christ also has forgiven you" (Vocabulary based on the American Standard Version). This is the life style of one who takes pleasure in accepting Bible bench marks because he loves God.

In my early teens I thought the Free Church was much too restrictive, but in adulthood I discovered the church has changed as it has matured. Is it not also that I matured? There is a positive dynamic for a life style which expresses itself in a freedom and power to please God.

The mother of John Wesley gave her son some sound advice when she said:

> Would you judge the lawfulness or the unlawfulness of pleasure? Take this rule: Whatever weakens your reason, impairs the tenderness of your conscience, obscures your sense of God, or takes off the relish of spiritual things—in short, whatever increases the strength and authority of your body over your mind, that thing is sin to you, however innocent it may appear in itself.[23]

FOOTNOTES—CHAPTER II

1. Adler, Alfred, 1870-1937.
2. Mavis, W. Curry, *Beyond Conformity*, Life and Light Press, Winona Lake, Ind., 1958, p. 58.
3. Ibid., p.58.
4. Jones, Rufus, *The Testimony of the Soul*, McMillan, New York, 1937, p. 203.
5. *The Golden Jubilee*, 1934, p. 29.
6. Moyer, Elgin S., *Who Was Who in Church History*, Moody Press, Chicago 1962, p. 384.
7. Ollen, P., Letter to brother O dated October 1876 published in *Paul Peter Waldenstrom*, a biography, p. 103.
8. Ibid., From a letter to the Swedish paper, *Göteborgs Veckoblad* in 1876, p. 109.
9. Carlsen, Nil C., *Liv og Virksomhed* i Herrens Vingaard, Evangelisten's Forlag, Chicago, 1928, p. 15, 16.
10. Shaw, Joseph M., *Pulpit Under the Sky*, Augsburg Publishing House, Minneapolis, 1955, pp. 4-5.
11. Ording, Hans N. H., *Hans Nielsen Hauge's Skrifter*, Oslo, 1947, II. p. 72.
12. *Golden Jubilee*, op. cit. p. 14.
13. Montgomery, Marcus W., *Winds of the Holy Spirit in Sweden and Norway*, American Home Missions Society, New York, 1884, p. 84.
14. *Golden Jubilee*, op. cit. p. 28, 29.
15. *Diamond Jubilee Story*, Free Church Publications, Minneapolis, 1959, p. 147.
16. Halleen, E. A., *Sunshine and Shadow*, Evangelical Beacon, Chicago, p. 104, 105.
17. Years later I had the honor of speaking at the funeral service for Mrs. Wedell. The story of the feather came to mind and I could not resist referring to a Chinese translation of I Peter 5:1. The language had no expression for "crown of glory" so they translated the expression, "a bright red hat that does not fade away." I reminded those in attendance of the Cardinal's red hat hanging from the ceiling of the cathedral only to turn black and disintegrate with time. Her hat would not fade!
18. National Religious Broadcaster statistics reported by Religious News Service, August 8, 1978.
19. McCombs, Phil., "Born Again Celebrities to Star at Broadcaster's Meeting," *Washington Post*, January 22, 1978.
20. Refkin, Jeremy and Howard, Ted, *The Emerging Order*, G. P. Putnam's and Sons, New York, 1979, p. 105.
21. Ibid., p. 106.
22. Published by permission of the author and Department of Church Ministries, Evangelical Free Church of America.
23. Townsend, Workman and Eayrs, *New History of Methodism*, Nashville, Methodist Episcopal Church, South, 1909, p. 63.

Chapter III

GROWING PAINS

The congregations born in the first and second decade of the first century of the existence of the Evangelical Free Church of America often began with a primitive form of church life—two or three gathered together in the name of Christ. This was enough to open the way for an itinerant evangelist, which in turn led to revivals that suddenly enlarged the group. The next step was the formation of Bible study and prayer fellowships often called Mission Societies, a term brought over from Scandinavia where, at that time, it was illegal to form congregations apart from the State Church.

Mission Societies are not to be confused with missionary organizations set up to send workers overseas. That developed when congregations agreed to work together in doing missionary work abroad. The local Mission Societies, in addition to meeting for prayer and Bible study, sought to evangelize the Scandinavians in the community. In this, the early believers were on the right track. To them, all believers were missionaries. One historian put it well when he wrote:

> Every Christian is naturally a missionary. He bears in his soul as an impelling command, the words: "Go ye into all the world and preach the Gospel to every creature." In the New Testament there is no distinction between clergy and laity, all saints are priests; so also there is no distinction between missionaries and non-missionaries, every believer is "sent" or has a "mission," to be a witness for Christ in the world.[1]

From Mission Societies the fellowships moved on to become loosely organized but incorporated congregations. This was forced upon them by two events. First, the new believers withdrew from the established churches. These were generally the Swedish, Norwegian and Danish Lutheran Synods. Second, to buy land and erect and own church buildings, it was necessary that the groups be incorporated.

Up to that point the assemblies had one thing in common, a factor which helped them overcome some problems and create others—*unorganized unity.* There was a unity of commitment to Christ and His Gospel. Both petitions in the prayer of Jesus as recorded in John 17, verse 21: "That they might be one . . . that the world may believe that thou hast sent me" were recognized.

But growth was slow and often painful. As the *Golden Jubilee* book put it: "All work among us made slow progress. To begin with, the churches could hardly be called organized congregations. No records were kept; no constitutions adopted; no prescribed method of work was followed."[2]

This lack of organization was to some a virtue; but to those who look back it was one of the reasons for the loss of much of the fruits of revival. Many were the stumbles enroute to maturity.

To fully understand the slow progress in the direction of organization one must again go back to the countries from which the believers had emigrated. They had grown up in nations in which the religious community was monolithic, only to find, on coming to America, that its religious community was pluralistic. The historic denominations, except for the Lutherans, were unknown to them. Revival movements among the English speaking citizens were on the other side of a distinct language barrier. Many had suffered hardship at the hands of organized religion in Denmark, Norway and Sweden where the State Churches controlled the religious life of the citizens. Membership in the church had been determined through baptism at earliest infancy and citizenship depended on it. Rules for church attendance and participation in communion were ordered by the church. Government appointed priests had instructed them as to what should be avoided. The Augsburg Confession was the law as far as Christianity was concerned.

The pioneers, therefore, were almost obsessed by two fears—the one based on ignorance and the other on experience. Not knowing any church organization other than the Lutheran, they would rather remain unorganized. Having experienced the devastating results of a dead orthodoxy forced upon them, they feared organization and insisted on freedom for the individual and independence for the group. Consequently many of the new fellowships died for lack of any method to preserve and consolidate the gains. Others, lacking means by which they could protect themselves against enemies from without, were splintered by fanaticism.

> Great waves of spiritual revivals have passed over these fields; waves of tempestuous storms as well. Due to the looseness of the organizations the free churches have been assailed by more disturbing forces from without than have most churches. Shrewd religious propagandists have found splendid soil in our field for their seditious seed. Our churches have been "free" churches in more ways than one. Both friends and foes have known this, and laid their plans accordingly.[3]

It is sad that in some places where revivals transformed entire communities, nothing remains except the names of the first generation engraved on tombstones. Reporting on the first fifty years of the Swedish Evangelical Free Church, the writer notes:

> The faith and trust in God that the sturdy pioneer possessed and exercised were somehow not transferred to the younger generation. Perhaps their faith was not transferable. At any rate a number of these small original churches are now

seldom used, some never. Even the little cemeteries alongside the churches seem forsaken. This is a pathetic sight. A strange loneliness creeps into the soul as one views these dilapidated monuments of a better day. The day of soul-saving labor is in these places a thing of the past. That is too bad. The day was so short. The sun set so soon—as it always does.

One cannot but wonder what happened to have caused all this. True spiritual zeal and fervor do not die of themselves. Empty churches are always a saddening and pathetic sight. They are a gruesome emblem of spiritual deterioration, an emblem of victory for the devil. And the saddest part of it is that it could have been avoided. There is no question as to that. In many cases it would have been avoided had there been a little more wisdom and tact blended with the fervor. Without wisdom fervor becomes a devastating fire. And it is a regrettable fact that a number of our former fields were actually burned out. Fanaticism was such a fire, that left death and hopelessness in its wake. Because of that one finds backsliders everywhere. That and godless young people and uninterested communities.

This is a sad fact; but a fact nevertheless. In nearly every place where fanaticism was permitted to run wild, the work suffered and gradually died out. On the other hand, wherever the work in its beginning was conducted along sound principles there are today strong and spiritual churches. Fanaticism is of the evil one. And the evil one is sure to be present at every spiritual awakening. Wherever the good seed is sown there will also be the tares. Life is always confronted with dangers. Spiritual life and its manifestations are not easily maintained. A carnal and fleshly liveliness can so easily take its place, and will, if the believers depend upon themselves instead of upon God. That tells the story in many places.[4]

The by-laws of one congregation stated that the pulpit was free and open to all who preached the Gospel except to those who represented an organization or belonged to a denomination. Thus an itinerant evangelist needed no credentials except his own recommendation. It is no surprise that the small congregation suffered many divisions through its early history.

One evangelist opposed to organization in the early years

was later to observe the fallacy of opposition:

> O how many small places there are where there have been
> revivals and where people lived well with God for a brief
> time. But then a false teacher arrived claiming to be a "free-
> preacher" (born again and non-denominational) who was ac-
> cepted without any credentials and proved to be not a
> shepherd but a wolf. It is sad even to think of the many
> sincere souls among the believers who have been thus de-
> ceived resulting in the laying down of the work. This is the
> result of the failure to consider the entire counsel of God in-
> cluding how a church should be organized.[5]

Opposition to organization was more prevalent among
the Swedes than among the Norwegians and Danes,
though national background had nothing to do with it. The
Swedish communities experienced great revivals, suddenly bringing into the Societies many babes in Christ who
turned against the churches to which they may have
belonged. The Norwegian-Danish congregations were
founded under the guidance and sponsorship of the Home
Mission Society of the Congregationalists which contributed, in addition to funds and leaders, three hundred
years of experience. This does not mean there were no
problems such as controversy over whether or not to adopt
creeds, organize nationally or merge the two associations
(Eastern and Western). But these were different than the
question of moving from Mission Societies to organized
congregations. In fact, they passed over that phase going
from the two or three gathered in Christ's name to locally
organized churches. As we have noted in the *Search for
Identity*, Chapter V, the early leaders were trained at the
Chicago Theological Seminary, the congregational school.[6]
In 1883, one year before the Norwegian-Danish Department was established, the Congregationalists adopted a
statement on the church which became the basis for the
local church structures. It was also similar to the one
adopted at the Boone conference in 1884, the difference
being that by that year the Swedish Free Church already

had a number of organized congregations and Mission Societies in their fellowship whereas the first Norwegian-Danish church was not organized (Scandinavian Congregational Church) until 1884.

The Congregational statement read:

X. We believe that the Church of Christ, invisible and spiritual, comprises all true believers, whose duty it is to associate themselves in churches, for the maintenance of worship, for the promotion of spiritual growth and fellowship, and for the conversion of men; that these churches, under the guidance of the Holy Scriptures in fellowship with one another, may determine—each for itself—their organization, statements of belief, and forms of worship, may appoint and set apart their own ministers, and should co-operate in the work which Christ has committed to them for the furtherance of the gospel throughout the world.[7]

The similarity between that and the one adopted in Boone is readily apparent:

4. Always remembering that the church is one in Christ: that He is the head of the church, and that the Holy Spirit is the infallible Leader into all truth: and that the Word of God, especially the New Testament, is the Constitution of the church and its *unforgettable* rule, therefore it behooves each group of believers to stand fast in the liberty wherewith Christ has made us free (Gal. 5:1); i.e. individually as well as collectively we have the right and obligation to remain independent of all forms of church authority, and to keep ourselves out of all obligations that might curtail such privileges and perfect liberty. But the local churches should therefore the more affiliate themselves by means of conferences and societies as well as with individuals in whom they have confidence. Note—that the local church has in accordance with the Word of God and the laws of our land, the right to ordain persons into Christian service, and these rights should be used in the fear of the Lord whenever so needed.[8]

The infant Mission Societies faced major problems in becoming organized congregations. What kind of church organization? What was the New Testament pattern?

Should it be a church under the authority of one person—episcopalian? Should it be under the authority of a committee—presbyterian? Should it be controlled entirely by the membership—congregational? The last of the three became the one accepted, but there were three additional problems in approaching the previously stated questions. Should a fellowship be based on membership—who would be the officers—what would be the role and authority of a pastor if one was called?

Before considering the questions of membership and ordination, a study of the *Modus Vivendi* of two of the pioneer leaders would be in order. It is a study of many contrasts and the consequences of the one believing strongly that the local group should be organized while the other had little time for such. They also had a number of things in common. Born the same year, both were evangelists mightily used of the Holy Spirit in far reaching revivals; both worked primarily in the Middle West—Iowa, Nebraska, the Dakota Territory and Minnesota; both worked among all the Scandinavians, and both were advocates of women as well as men preaching the Gospel. To them neither the gifts of the Spirit nor the Great Commission were based on the sex of the followers of Christ. But here the similarity ended. We refer to the Swede, Fredrik Franson (1852-1908) and the Dane, Nils C. Carlsen (1852-1932).

Franson was born in Sweden in 1852 to an evangelical, pietistic, Free Church-minded home. His mother started a women's missionary society and was active in the revival movement. When the Swedish Parliament repealed the Conventicle edict in 1858, she remodeled the second floor of her home to serve as an assembly place for the Bible Readers. Comparatively Franson had a good education. He completed four years of middle school and the first year of high school, having excelled in such subjects as Greek, Latin, German, mathematics, theology and Swedish.

His parents were in mining and farming but fell on ill times economically so liquidated the business. Young

Franson, by then seventeen, emigrated with his parents and three of his syblings to America, settling on homestead land in Nebraska. He was converted during a long, serious illness at the age of twenty.

Carlsen was born in Denmark into a poor, irreligious, peasant family in 1852. He grew up under deplorable economic conditions and religiously it was equally deplorable as noted in the preceding chapter. There wasn't even a Bible in the home. His parents sent the annual Christmas donation with others so as not to go near the church. Christmas was noted by drinking. He never saw nor heard anyone pray in his home. His mother attended Carlsen's confirmation exercises and, so far as he recalled, it was the first time she had been in church since his younger brother had been baptized. He married while still in Denmark. In 1878, at the age of 25, he, together with his wife, emigrated to america settling on land in the Dakota Territory. He arrived there with a New Testament in his possession having received it as a gift when entering the United States—as did all immigrants at that time. Both he and his wife were converted in 1880. Upon the realization that they were the only believers in the church, they withdrew from membership.

Although neither man had any theological education, and Carlsen, especially, a bare minimum of secular training, both were endowd with a wisdom that greatly exceeded knowledge. Both attended the "school of Jesus," studied the Word, and were under the tutelage of the Holy Spirit. Each possessed that added dimension which could have insured success in any field of endeavor. How these two were converted and became evangelists is an interesting story in itself but not pertinent to this report.

Franson, from the beginning of his ministry, revealed an insight about church organization along with the New Testament pattern and had valuable experience in the early years of his Christian life in church administration. His first exposure was in a small Baptist Church which was experiencing a revival. The church was host to the Second Annual meeting of the Scandinavian Missionary Association which had missionaries in Minnesota, Nebraska and the Dakotas—more exposure for the twenty-two-year-old Christian. On October 3, 1874, he was elected as secretary to serve on a council to decide whether or not to give recognition to a new Baptist Church. Later (June, 1875) at the age of 23 he was elected secretary of the Scandinavian Baptist Conference of Nebraska, Western Iowa and Dakota. He began his preaching ministry under the guidance of a veteran and gifted preacher traveling to towns in Nebraska.

Torjesen wrote that there followed a period of mystery beginning in the fall of 1875 when he seems to have dropped out of the Baptist scene reappearing sixteen months later as "a full-fledged evangelist." "His impact was soon felt in all four of the Lutheran synods as well as among the Baptists and Methodists. He showed a remarkable combination: a breadth of evangelical thinking, a depth of Scriptural insight, a knack for communicating with the common people and a personal morality which held his life and work and his professed faith in Christ in an unassailable harmony. This blending of traits was not only staggering, but it commanded respect from friend and foe alike."[9]

No one has done more complete research on the life and work of Franson than has Edvard P. Torjesen, who reported he found that no primary sources seemed to exist from this period. The secondary sources support the view that he was a student of Dwight L. Moody at that time although he didn't join the church in Chicago until August 4, 1878. He may have accompanied Moody in his campaigns in Brooklyn, Philadelphia, and Manhatten and studied and worked in them.[10] We do know that he was a keen observer and a fast learner.

Upon his return to the Midwest, after his months of absence, he also seems to have broken his Swedish Baptist connections. His first documented public appearance was in Swede Bend, Iowa, in February of 1977. From then on he worked more and more with the groups that would eventually become Swedish Evangelical Free Churches.

Franson was a churchman, a quality sometimes overlooked by those who think of him only as an overseas missionary leader. His early experience in church administration and the knowledge gained at the Moody Church in Chicago served him well. While not unmindful of his missionary endeavors, the Evangelical Free Church of America, as well as those in Scandinavia and even in Germany, are greatly indebted to him for his contribution to the structuring of the local churches.

He did this in two ways—by writing articles in the Swedish paper, *Chicago Bladet,* on the New Testament pattern for the local church, and by visiting local mission societies and Bible study groups to help them organize as churches. The first of many such articles appeared on May 23, 1879, entitled, *A Contribution to the Solution of the Complicated Denominational and Local Church Question.* Many other articles on the same subject followed.

Although he had assisted in the organizing of two works in Utah, his first accomplishment among what was to become the core of the Swedish Evangelical Free Church meeting in Boone in 1884, was the church in Denver on July 16, 1880. There followed in rapid succession similar organizational meetings at Phelps Center on November 16, Westmark on the 19th, Industry on the 23rd and Keene on the 25th—all located in Nebraska. In each case, Franson was chosen to chair the meeting.

Inspired and enlightened by what he had seen, read, and heard on the subject of church organization in Chicago, Franson proceeded to follow the pattern of the Moody Church. His philosophy is reflected in what he wrote following the meeting in Denver.

> They consider that differing concepts about points not vital to the life in Christ ought not to hinder in any way brotherly love

or the extension of full brotherly fellowship. Consequently, they have left to each individual believer such questions as, for instance, the various doctrines about the mode, time and meaning of baptism, so that on those questions each member may believe and act in accordance with his own best understanding of the Word of God without having to feel even the slightest alienation from his fellow believers in the flock.[11]

Baptism was another doctrine in which the two men who influenced the thinking in the new churches agreed. Carlsen, slower to recognize the problem and its solution, wrote following his orientation to the Norwegian-Danish congregations:

I love the Evangelical Free Church since, in accord with my understanding, the structure comes as close to the Word of God and the teaching of the apostles as possible. I wish it had existed when I first started my work as a preacher. First, I like its confession of faith . . . In the second place, the congregation accepts no member unless he has experienced personal salvation and lives in fellowship with God. Likewise, they practice discipline . . . Pastors are called by the congregations to be servants of the church. The third is that the Free Church recognizes freedom of conscience regarding the method of baptism. Even in Paul's time there were different views as to certain matters. Some still held to circumcision and even Paul had Timothy circumcised. If one wished to quarrel, there is enough "stuff" available. But we do not follow that custom.[12]

The conviction that the church was for believers only but open to all believers existed long before the book *Believers Only* was written![13]

The basic principles of organization in each case were identical with those adopted by the Moody Church in Chicago fifteen years earlier. They were also similar to those eventually adopted by the early congregations of the Norwegian-Danish Association since they came from a common root—American Congregationalism.

The Swedish community was greatly influenced by Dwight L. Moody. His sermons were reported in the *Chicago Bladet*. Immigrants had also read of him in the old country and were familiar with the songs of Sankey. The

Swedes, in large numbers, attended his meetings in Chicago. In recognition of this fact, the congregation in 1873 called a pastor to minister to the Scandinavians.

Many hundreds of Swedes became acquainted with Moody and his church almost from the first day and remained there. They soon became thoroughly Americanized and today their children and grandchildren make up perhaps half the membership (1938).[14]

Because of the impact of the Moody Church principles of organization on the development of local congregations among the Swedes it might be well to digress from the story of the growing pains of the Free Churches to consider the growing pains of the Chicago church. These have been well documented in books published as early as 1876, four years before the churches in Colorado and Nebraska were organized and eight years before the first Scandinavian Congregational Churches were started in Tacoma, Washington, and Boston, Massachusettes.

Dwight L. Moody, member of a Congregational Church and the Y.M.C.A., began his preaching ministry while a shoe salesman. God blessed his work so abundantly that he gave up secular employment. He recommended to the converts that they join the communions in which they had been brought up, but there were many who could not be identified with any church.

The most of these had no religious antecedents whatever. Some of them came from a depth of heathenism so far below the Church of God that, of its forms, orders, and divisions, they knew and cared absolutely nothing. But there was a strong tie binding them to each other which it was found impossible to transfer to any other body of worshippers. They had come up together out of poverty and ignorance; they had learned their duty in the same school, and under the same teacher; and thus their fellowship of suffering, as well as their fellowship of faith, was something with which no stranger might intermeddle.

It must also be confessed that, of all the Christian congregations then in Chicago, there was not one to whose care these persons, who had nothing to commend them except the fact that they were saved sinners, could safely be confided. The very reasons for which they needed sympathy and attention were those which would prevent them from receiving it. Thus the necessity for a church of their own became increasingly evident.[15]

From the beginning Moody sought to cooperate with the existing churches but the pastors stood aloof. During the Civil War, however, as they worked with him among the victims, they developed a new respect and even affection for him. Moody, too, was a churchman.

> That religious conceit, whose father is Zeal and whose mother is Ignorance, and which is so often found in the heads of men who come to sudden success outside of the organized Church, was not found in Mr. Moody. He never doubted the value of the ministry of the Churches in any forms they had adopted. But none of these forms could meet the needs of his particular congregation. Therefore, after much prayer for Divine guidance, he invited all the city ministers of his acquaintance, with a number of prominent laymen, to meet in council, at the Illinois Street Chapel, for the purpose of organizing a Christian communion for the three hundred people who had been converted under his ministry.[16]

The council met in December of 1864. Represented at that meeting by their pastors were Episcopal, Presbyterian, Methodist, Baptist and Congregational Churches. The question under consideration was one which was to become familiar to the Scandinavians a few years later. If we are to organize, what type of church structure should it be? As the council met, they had before them a plan drafted as a result of an earlier meeting.

Moody, who opened the meeting, explained how he had failed in his efforts to bring many of the converts at the Mission into existing congregations and stressed the importance of organizing a church with himself as pastor which might be recognized in Christian circles. His goal, as stated in the remarks, was to "form an orderly congregation of believers, among whom the ordinance of the Gospel should be celebrated and the work of the Lord carried on."

As he continued explaining the plan, leaders of the various churches representing different forms of church structures withdrew one by one. First, the rector of the Episcopal congregation withdrew because, though he supported Moody's work, he found the plan incompatible with the episcopal structure. Likewise, a Presbyterian pastor, also sympathetic, told the meeting that he could not help in organizing a church unless it was in accord with a presbyterian form of church government. A Baptist could not support the plan because the man who was to be the pastor (Moody) had been sprinkled not immersed. A Methodist pastor felt that it could not be organized along Methodist lines which also was episcopal in church structure. Furthermore, since Moody held to some of the points of Calvinism, a Methodist congregation, being Arminian, would be inconsistent and introduce additional conflicts.

With all of these eliminated, the Congregationalists were the only ones left, and accepted with a sense of satisfaction the task of organizing The Illinois Street Church, "since their method excelled all others on this notable occasion. It was the only one simple enough to meet the wants of this peculiar people whose only notion of a church was a company of saved sinners with Mr. Moody for their pastor and Jesus Christ as Head over all."[17]

This reminds us of what another historian wrote at about the same time:

Wherever any company of persons may be, who are faithful believers in the Gospel, and who desire to bless themselves and serve Christ in and through a Church organization, they may do so in a Congregational form, without any perplexity or delay. They do not need to geographise and journey, to discover some well authenticated aqueduct, bringing the stream of Ecclesiastical life down from the hoary past, to which they must attach themselves, or else be dry; they may dig down anywhere in the sand, with the certainty of finding living water. Suppose they are grouped upon some far Pacific slope, hundreds of miles from any Church, of any name, with communication almost interdicted by the distance and peril of the way; if they are to become Papal, Patriarchal, Episcopalian, Methodist, or Presbyterian in their spirit and form of Church organization, they must wait and work until they can put themselves into communication with the rest of the world, so as to get hold of the arm of that particular hierarchy which they prefer, and procure its extension to their remote locality, with all due conditions and ceremonies, for such cases made and provided. All this involves delay, trouble, expense; often disappointment and dispersion. Moreover, in its very nature, this necessity of going so far for, and making so much of, mere forms, must tend to magnify forms unduly, and turn their thoughts away from the simplicity of Christ. Still further they are, even when formed, abnormal and incomplete; lacking the aid, for the perfect doing of all their work, of the distant Pope, Bishop, or Presbytery.

But if they wish to become a Congregational Church, they can become such, there by themselves, in a single hour—by solemn vote affiliating for that purpose, and adopting our simple creed . . . Such a Church, on our principles, is just as perfect in its order, as it could be if all the other churches in the world had helped to make it. It is just as near to Christ, as, and it may be a little nearer than, any other—as the babe lies closer to its mother's breast than the older children. He is just as really its Head, and it is just as truly the channel of his power and grace, as the grandest metropolitan Church can be. And there, in its outward feebleness, and in that remoteness, its voice is just as imperative as that of the oldest and numerically strongest body of congenial faith on earth; because Christ says, that "where two or three are," there he will be, and because the comforting and controlling Spirit can dwell in a little Church just as well as in a large one. And so there it stands—home-made and yet well made—as true a Church as the Great Head anywhere surveys. There it can advance from strength to strength, burdened with no extraneous connections or responsibilities; going to the Bible with humble prayer, and not to General Conference, Convention, or Assembly, to find out what shall be its creed, and what its life. So soon as the growth of a community around it shall evoke the element of the fellowship of the saints, it will affiliate with other Congregational churches as any shall grow up within its neighborhood; and then its entire completeness of relation, without as well as within, will be secured.

There is another feature of the superior practicableness of the Congregational system in the formation of new churches, which was illustrated in the early days of Christianity, and which is now particularly commended to our attention by the present and prospective condition of our own country. It consists in its freedom from all embarrassment in regard to form, where questions of would be embarrassing; and in its freedom from all entangling alliances and inconvenient precedents, and awkward responsibilities, growing out of the relations of a rigid and wide spread organism to the past. If our Saviour had instituted a technical Church system, having a necessary embodiment in certain usages, and by certain officers, and through certain far reaching relations—a centralized administration with executive branches—its progress would have excited hostility at every step, for it could have taken no step without colliding with existing organizations, social, Ecclesiastical, civil. But a development of Christianity which presented a *faith* to be believed rather than a *form* to be adopted, could glide in between all barriers, and establish itself noiselessly as an *imperium in imperio* everywhere; subsequently embodying its recipients according to local convenience, and perfecting their Church character and relation—and so their thorough organic union to the Great Head—without the need of conspicuous and obnoxious publicity, and premature positive conflict with the things that were.[18]

Dexter's book was published in 1874, two years prior to the book by Daniels on the Life and Work of Moody. Both were available to the leaders in 1880 and the former was one of the texts available to the pastors of the Norwegian-Danish Churches who studied at the Chicago Theological Seminary beginning in 1875.

Returning to the story of the Moody Church which was organized as the Illinois Street Church, the name later changed to the Chicago Avenue Church, we find that the statements in the Articles of Faith and the Principles of Organization and Government reveal again how carefully Franson followed that pattern in organizing Evangelical Free Churches. Though the articles of faith are composed entirely of verses from the Scriptures, the creed concludes with an explanation:

> In accepting and subscribing to the above articles of faith, we
> by no means set aside or undervalue any of the Scriptures of
> the Old and New Testament, but believe all to be equally
> God's own written Word, given to us through the inspiration
> of the Holy Spirit; but the knowledge and belief of the truth,
> as stated in our articles of faith, we deem necessary to salva-
> tion and sound doctrine, and thereby requisite for Christian
> fellowship.

The similarity to Franson's position also appears in the
declaration of principles.

> This body of believers desires to be known only as Christians,
> without reference to any denomination; yet regarding all who
> hold and preach the truth contained in our articles of faith as
> equally belonging to the same Head; and are thereby free to
> cooperate and unite with them in carrying on the work of our
> common Master.

> The government is vested in the body of believers of which
> the Church is composed.

One need but read from the Articles of Incorporation of the
Denver congregation filed on July 27, 1880, to discover the
Moody Church pattern. In fact, they are identical.

There is another matter of interest that should be noted
before leaving the story of the organization in Chicago and
its influence on the Evangelical Free Church early congregations. Though organized by the Congregationalists,
the Moody Church has never been reckoned as a Congregational Church by that denomination. The historian
wrote:

> Its minister has received no ordination, save that of the Spirit
> and Providence of God; his name has never been published in
> the minutes of that body or any other; and the statistics of the
> society have never been published at all. It is a strictly in-
> dependent organization, asking no authority of men, but
> abundantly blessed of the Lord it endeavors to keep the unity
> of the Spirit in the bond of peace; and, with this end in view,
> everything which could debar from its fellowship any lover of
> the Lord Jesus Christ has been carefully excluded from its

form of discipline and confession of faith.[19]

We now turn to the second leader introduced at the beginning of this chapter; namely, Nils C. Carlsen. Early in his career he definitely was not a churchman! His experiences in Denmark as well as with two different denominational churches he had joined in America, from which he later resigned, removed any interest in organizing the many new converts into churches. He discouraged it. This was a grievous error on his part. By the time he wrote his autobiography in 1928 he had discovered his mistake and confessed it, but much of the potential long-term gains for the cause of Christ and His Church had been irretrievably lost.

But Carlsen was not alone in his opposition to organization. One must remember, too, that in the first years he confined his work to the Dakotas, Minnesota, Iowa, Wisconsin and Nebraska and had little, if any, contact with the Norwegian-Danish Evangelical Free Churches in Illinois and on the East Coast, which had been organized under the auspices of the American Congregational Society. His first contacts with the Swedish Free groups were Mission Societies and young congregations.

His early experiences with the established churches of the historic denominations was enough in itself to turn him against any form of organization. It was also a time when he found support for his position among the Swedish groups because they were in the process of going through growing pains. For example, he wrote of visiting believers in Cherokee, Alta, Storm Lake, Meriden, Meriton, etc., in Iowa. In all of these places the societies kept no membership records. In other words, all the believers were "members." One of these congregations in Iowa still has no membership and considers it a virtue!

He also met a group of believers north of Beresford, South Dakota. The work had begun in 1873-1874 and, though some persons were designated as elders and others as deacons, it had no formal membership list. "This," they said, "is what the world does." They claimed further, that God keeps the record of membership. As an indication of his own philosophy at that time, Carlsen accepted the invitation to fellowship with this society. The brethren were meeting in a schoolhouse near his home. Prior to securing a schoolhouse they met in dugouts and private homes. The Beresford Church, organized in 1883, has been a strong, supportive congregation of the Evangelical Free Church of America since its beginning in 1884. There was an element of organization which may have contributed to their survival during the early years.

An indication of the importance of organization is readily apparent in the study of the long-term results of Franson's work and the lack of same following Carlsen's revivals. For example, we find that there were revivals in such places as Wiborg, Turkey Creek, Lake Preston, Langford, Arlington, Stockholm, Brookings, Dell Rapids and Baltic in South Dakota; Lime Creek, Minden, Hardington, Wakefield, Concord and Oakland in Nebraska; Thief River Falls, Fosston, Windom and Sleepy Eye in Minnesota; and Chippewa Falls in Wisconsin. These are but a few. Some of the names are familiar communities in which Free Churches are located today but these were either congregations before Carlsen was there or started many years later as new works under the auspices of the Board of Home Missions. Carlsen's method was to win converts to Christ and then leave them without any program to care for the new flock.

He confessed his error early in his autobiography. "My fellow workers and I had no experience in such things and further, had given no thought to the matter of organizing a Biblically based congregation or to encouraging the new converts to join a congregation coming closest to the Scriptural pattern. We, ourselves, belonged to no congregation and we consequently believed that once a person was saved these other matters would take care of themselves. This was a mistake on our part since the Word of God clearly teaches that the apostles organized congregations which naturally were not composed of non-believers but of believers only."[20]

The change in his attitude developed after he had been exposed to the organized Evangelical Free Churches on the East Coast. Carlsen was a keen observer and a student. He could be led to change a viewpoint once convinced that the matter of church structure was not only Scriptural but practical. His first visit was in 1900 to hold meetings in the Norwegian Evangelical Free Church in Brooklyn. He had heard rumors that the churches were worldly and that the pastors had to be the same to keep their calls. He wrote following that first visit, "Not all one hears is true. I found conditions the opposite of what I had heard. They had come much farther in many ways in the East than in the West."[21]

He was invited back to the East Coast in 1903 and accepted with pleasure and anticipation for two reasons. "There was a better order of church organization and less strife than in the West. Further, there were many young people sensing a call to preach the Gospel. These, I might encourage."[22]

On that trip he visited the churches in Jersey City, Hoboken, West Orange, New Haven and Hartford, as well as Brooklyn. "I became more and more convinced that the organization of churches was better but the question was, how could I introduce similar principles in the West?" [23]

On his third visit (1907) he served the Brooklyn Church as interim for three months. In 1910 he was East again. The churches, he discovered, had officers, Sunday Schools, youth groups, etc. Discipline was practiced. Money was raised systematically on "the first day of the week" in accordance with the Scriptures. The members conducted the business of the church at regular and special business meetings. He also served as pastor of the congregation on Staten Island for a year beginning on March 1, 1914. This was his postgraduate course in church administration.

From then on Carlsen was a new man in his attitude towards and understanding of church and denominational organization and became a strong leader in the Norwegian-Danish Evangelical Free Church Association. In 1928 he could look back and see the tragedy of his mistakes in the early years:

> As one looks out over the great fields of the West and the people who live there and recalls the many years of labor and sacrifices laid down together with the many revivals, not only as the results of my work but also that of others—both brothers and sisters—who gave up good homes to die in poverty; then when one sees the conditions today (1928) one cannot help but be filled with sadness.
>
> If we had only said to the new converts, "Now we will follow the Scriptures also as they deal with a congregation's organization even though we are few." If we had only found someone to take care of the flock, watch over it, not for personal gain but out of love, how different matters would have been today. This has frequently come before me. Recently, I have often felt like Jeremiah the prophet: "Oh that my head were waters, and mine eyes a fountain of tears, that I might weep day and night for the slain of the daughter of my people!" Jeremiah 9:1-2.
>
> It is certainly good to have one's eyes opened before it is too late and to know that God will forgive us the mistakes made in good faith.[24]

In recalling the small groups having no membership records but who considered all as members, he wrote in retrospect:

> There developed a collective responsibility. In those days people were as afraid of personal responsibility as they were afraid of the evil one. As long as the revival continued and they were burning in the spirit all went well. But when difficulties arose, even as in the time of the apostles, they were without counsel. The Epistles are surely given for our learning. Therefore we can know how a Christian congregation should be organized; who should be accepted or rejected for membership; and the qualifications for leadership.[25]

So Carlsen eventually, over a long tortuous route, came

to the same conclusion as did Franson.

There is one interesting conviction common to both from the beginning of their ministry; namely, the role of women in the work of evangelism. Carlsen encouraged women to preach and assisted them in every way possible. The list of these women is long as is also the list of those trained by Franson for work at home and overseas. Both put their views in writing.

Carlsen, in his autobiography, not only told of their work but declared his position in several of the chapters. He wrote, for example, of meeting two women evangelists, Hilma Sivrin and Mary Madsen, in Nebraska at a time when they were despondent. They found themselves in unforeseen circumstances and with their funds depleted. They met preachers who declared that when women preached God's Word they were sowing stolen seed.

> It was my view then and remains unchanged today that it makes no difference whom God uses as His instrument—it is only that sinners are saved through the blood of Jesus and kept by His grace. It makes no difference to me whether the Lord uses men or women, Lutherans or Methodists, Quakers or Baptists, Free Church people or someone from another denomination—just so people do not die in their sins.[26]

Franson wrote a pamphlet on the subject entitled, *Prophesying Daughters.* It was first published in German in 1887 and in Swedish in 1897. In it he traces the role of women in both the Old Testament and the New. The entire treatise is based on the theme of the pioneers, "Where stands it written?" "There is no prohibition in the Bible," he wrote, "against women serving Christ in public. We face the situation that the devil, fortunately for him, has succeeded in excluding nearly two-thirds of the number of Christians from participation in the Lord's service through evangelization. The damage to God's cause is so great as to be indescribable. The fields of labor are large, and when we realize that nearly two-thirds of all converted peopel in the world are women, then the question of the role of women in evangelism is of great importance."

He insisted that the spiritual gifts should be used regardless of whether the one having the gift is a man or a woman.

When we come to the time that Jesus Himself ministered on the earth, we find that he declared with all certainty that each one must employ his gifts (his pound) which he has received and threatens all with serious punishment who hide their pound in a cloth. Now, when a woman has a gift to be an evangelist, how can she dare avoid employing such a gift. For each of God's children it should be clear that God continually requires that we do all we can for Him. When you have responsibilities which require your time in summer, use the winter for God. When you can make use of all your time directly in the Lord's work, do it. If you cannot prophesy (proclaim) then pray; but if you can do both, so much the better. Many ask whether there will not be altogether too many workers and messengers. This is a point that can be considered after all the heathen have been converted or at least have heard the Gospel; but until that has happened there are altogether too few and not too many who have gone forth. That a sister can equally well serve God in her secular work can be true, but it can equally well be false. If she has been led into an earthly calling, she can even so be a true servant of Christ. If she is faithful in her calling as it is stated in Ephesians 6:7, that even such "serve the Lord." But if, on the contrary, she has the gifts of an evangelist and nothing hinders her from using her full time for the Lord, then it is not possible for her to serve the Lord just as acceptably in her earthly calling, at least as long as there are over 50,000,000 people who each year go into eternity, of whom most have not even heard one word concerning salvation in Jesus.

In support of his position he considered thirty-nine passages of Scripture, some covering entire chapters, and reviewed the work of eighteen women of the Bible.

He also found support from the writings of Martin Luther:

Luther, the reformer, had the same interpretation, namely that women should speak. In one of his pastoral letters to Bohemian brethren where he speaks against the papacy, he points out that in the word in I Peter 2:9, "Ye are a chosen generation, a royal priesthood, and a holy nation, a people of His own, that ye should show forth the praises of Him who called you out of darkness into his marvelous light" are not written only for the hereditary priesthood but for the entire congregation. He says explicitly, "each and every one of God's children, women, included, has the right to administer the Word, baptism and communion."

In many ways, Franson was a man ahead of his times. In contrasting the way society uses the gifts and abilities of women, neglected by the church, he wrote:

The first place in the Bible which speaks about a woman tells us that she shall be "a help" to her husband. If she was created to be a suitable help to man in temporal matters, why not also in the spiritual? If she is now so often a help, for example, as teacher in the public schools, why not also a teacher for the heathen and the unconverted in general? Since she is permitted to practice as a physician, why not then as a physician for souls? When she is able to use her gifts in the service of sin as in the theater, etc., why can she not use her influence for the benefit of the Lord who created her. As we more and more recognize her gifts and influence in secular areas, why not also in the spiritual? Furthermore, since she helped to bring sin and evil into the world, why should she not be allowed to help in every way she can to rid the world of sin? When she had, for example, so great influence on her husband for evil, namely to get him to take of the forbidden fruit, why not also use her influence over men as well as over her own sisters in order to please the Saviour?[27]

In addition to growing pains over organization and membership there was the matter of ordained, resident, financially supported pastors.

In the beginning the societies were served occasionally by itinerant evangelists and teachers. These were sometimes "invited by the Holy Spirit" without the Spirit having informed the brethren! Many fellowships were led by lay *leaders* often called elders. A *ruling* elder would have been an anathema to them. They had experienced problems in the old countries with government appointed clergymen and were slow to consider resident pastors. For example, the congregation at Denver, organized in 1880, was served for seven years by a layman—a shoemaker named Nels Johnson—before a pastor was called.

The itinerant evangelists were preachers rather than pastors. As the *Golden Jubilee* book states, "In the beginning very few churches had pastors. And none were given that title. As a matter of fact the ministers themselves prohibited the use of any designating title. It was 'brother so and so' and nothing else. And that was sufficient. Every preacher was more or less a traveling missionary, and all were evangelists by the grace of God."[28] In other words, by the grace of God only and not by any local church or other religious establishment. This custom contributed to the development of gifts in the local congregation:

> The Elders of the churches had charge of the services whenever there were no preachers at hand. This method developed many local gifts in the churches. The success of the respective churches depended to a large extent upon the local talents. Hence prayer, testimony and singing were common in all the churches. The lay-element has therefore in that respect been prominent so far as the local church work is concerned. And it has been of great blessing to our work, especially in the early and formative period. This method created also an intense hunger for the knowledge of the Word of God. The need of knowing what the Bible teaches created in the pioneers an interest that nothing could quench. They wanted to know just what they believed. And they wanted to have this knowledge independent of established doctrines and beliefs. They wanted to be guided by no other book than the Bible. This independence, so good and worthy in itself, developed, however, a "cock-sureness" that in many instances became detrimental to the work.

> This method continued for approximately twenty years. The writer entered into the work ten years after the Free Church was organized, and there were at that time in the state of Minnesota only two or three churches that had a pastor. All the other churches were visited off and on by traveling ministers. As a rule these traveling preachers would travel in pairs. One would be older and more experienced; the other young and a beginner. Or one would be more gifted for preaching, and the

other for singing. Both of these combinations worked admirably well, because the churches were more or less in need of this variety of gifts.[29]

One should note that there is a very thin line between maturity and senility. The pioneers did not enjoy a forty hour week or modern farm equipment and yet gave time as well as money to the work of the church. Checks are no substitute for time. The stewardship of time is as important as the stewardship of money. The Corinthians were able to give beyond their means because "they first gave themselves to the Lord and to us by the will of God" (2 Corinthians 8:5). With the increasing tendency to change the membership from participants to spectators by hiring more and more staff, the people lose the joy of service and the challenge to the study of God's Word. This lack of exercise fosters hardening of the spiritual arteries. The lay activity of the early days had its advantages.

The question of ordination also had to be settled. Their experiences in the Scandinavian countries contributed to their hesitancy. Only the State Churches had the authority to ordain. In America an ordination by a local church would be recognized by the government as authorizing the person thus ordained to perform marriages on behalf of the local government and it even granted them a fifty percent discount on the railroads. But there was still the lingering fear that such ordained persons would assume the same kind of authority from which they had escaped by emigrating to the United States. One often used argument was that, "Dwight L. Moody was not ordained and just look at how God is using him." Carlsen and Franson did much to prepare the way to an acceptance of ordination by themselves accepting such credentials. Franson, as we have documented, was a churchman from the beginning. Before he went forth as an evangelist he was careful to have a proper certificate of recognition by a church body. This was provided by the Executive Committee of the Moody Church on August 4, 1878, the very day he joined the congregation.

TO WHOM IT MAY CONCERN

The bearer, Rev. F. Franson, having won our confidence during the time he has been among us (he being a member of our church) and going forth now in evangelistic work, we commend him to the Lord and to the Lord's people wherever his labors call him.[30]

The recommendation was signed by F. H. Revell.

Franson also wrote about his views on ministerial credentials:

We recognize, of course, that it is the Holy Spirit who in the first place gives license or authority to preach. Nevertheless, it is both well and necessary that an evangelist who goes out to witness about the Lord, has his local church's recommendation that he is a brother in Christ as well as a worker in the vineyard. We find, for instance, that the apostles wrote such letters both for the purpose of recommending (as in I Corinthians 16:10, Colossians 4:10, Romans 16:1-2, and III John 1:5-8) and for the purpose of warning (as in II Timothy 2:17, 4:15, and III John 1:9-10). [31]

When Franson was making plans to visit Sweden, he received the following letter from Mr. Emil Olson, Secretary of the Board of the Phelps Center congregation:

It has occurred to us that if you go to Sweden, it will become all the more important for you to have formal ordination by a church. We know you have credentials from the Chicago Avenue Church, and I have read them. They will do here in America, but you know how particular the state church is over there. We believe it would be appropriate for you to be ordained to the gospel ministry, and we would rejoice if the ordination could be here in this church which you yourself helped organize.[32]

He wrote of his response in the article published in *Chicago Bladet*, December 17, 1880:

The laying on of hands accompanied by the prayers to God of his children is something that brings a great blessing with it. As I took part in calling down God's blessing on the elders in the Phelps church, I could not help but wish—as a brother in

Minnesota had once said—"Surely, this is something I need every time I go to preach." Therefore, even though twice before I had been set apart through the laying on of hands by God's children, I could not help asking now that these elders set me apart for the third time.

They did this when I was about to leave, and the elders together with the whole congregation of God's children joined together in prayer for me that God's blessing might rest on me wherever He might lead me.[33]

The offer from Phelps Center was readily accepted as it was supported by what he had found in the study of the Scriptures. The ordination took place on January 20, 1881. His response upon receiving the certificate of ordination was, "I will treasure this document, but I will treasure even more the prayers you have offered in my behalf. I believe that your action is recorded not just here but in the books of heaven."[34]

The very next weekend he was in Chicago to preach in the Moody Church. When he shared the news of his ordination, he was told, "We would have been glad to do the same for you." He responded, "I know that, and I considered it. After prayer I felt it would mean a tremendous lot to the Phelps Center people and to myself at the end of my ministry among them. That is why I was ordained there, but I still hold my membership in our Chicago Avenue Church. This is my home base."[35]

Carlson was ordained at a mission meeting held in the church at Concord, Nebraska, on July 14, 1895. Because of his later association with the Norwegian-Danish group it is of interest that he should have been ordained in one of the Swedish congregations. He wrote, "In one way, I had been set apart for the work of evangelism, but in accordance with the legal requirements that a man be ordained by a church so authorized, my conscience had often troubled me that I had not sought such credentials. So I accepted that opportunity to have it done."[36]

There could also well have been a sentimental reason for

having this ordination take place at Concord. The congregation traces its origin back to 1892 when "Rev. Fred Nelson and Rev. Nils Carlsen held meetings there." These resulted in a revival and the conversion of about forty souls.[37] Like Franson, he accepted ordination from a flock whom he had fathered and with whom he had worked. In both cases it also revealed a recognition of the authority of the local church to ordain.

The laws to which he referred hastened to remove opposition by the churches to ordination. Without it, no marriage could be performed since, in such a rite, the one officiating was a servant of the government as well as the church. The form to be signed was not a religious but a secular, legal document.

Once the hesitancy to ordaining workers was overcome, it should come as no surprise following the teachings and examples of Carlsen and Franson that women as well as men were ordained. A number of revivals leading to the establishment of organized congregations were the result of the work of women preachers.

Again, it might be in order to mention that the problems of ministerial standing and the role of pastors was in some ways peculiar to the Swedish Evangelical Free Church. The Norwegian-Danish Association escaped these particular growing pains. Many of the pastors were missionaries supported by the American Home Missions Society and held credentials provided by the Congregationalists. One should also recall that the history of the Swedish problems goes much farther back in time. By the year that the pastors of the Swedish churches were able to organize the Ministerial Association (1894) the Norwegian-Danish Churches were still nearly twenty years away from a formal organization nationally.

One difference developed in the ordination procedure which had to be reconciled before the merger of the two denominations could be considered in 1950. It is clear from Franson's statement that in his opinion the local congregation should grant the ministerial credentials. Further, his ordination was by a local church. But this was four years before the Swedish congregations joined in the mutual work in 1884. Authority of the local church to ordain was clearly stated in the Boone document. As time went on, there was an apparent shift from local ordinations to ordinations by and at the national conferences. The Norwegian-Danish Association on the other hand, held to the policy introduced in the report of the Congregational Commission on December 19, 1883, including the right of local churches to call and ordain their own pastors.

The procedure was followed until the merger. Local congregations would call an ordination council, invite neighboring Evangelical Free Churches to send representatives, examine the candidate and if advisable proceed with the act of laying on of hands and the extension of the right hand of fellowship. The examination was usually public and held in the afternoon. While the council deliberated in private following the examination, the local congregation served supper to all the guests. The public ordination service followed. It's interesting that no provision was made for a possible rejection of the candidate. The vote was not always unanimous, as would have been especially true during a period of controversy over some doctrine. I recall one incident when two pastors, suspicious of the candidate's views on "eternal security," remained seated in the front row in protest as the rest of the council went to the platform for the laying on of hands. The bright lights overhead reflecting off their bald heads accentuated the negative!

The compromise in the merger plan offers another evidence of maturity. The local congregation retains the right to call and ordain anyone it chooses. However, the credentials thus made available are not necessarily recognized by other churches. To obtain national recognition the candidate, though ordained in a local church by a council called by the congregation, is previously approved as a candidate by a Committee on Ministerial Standing. The rules also include the procedure for the revocation of ordination.

For an interesting and illuminating example of growing pains we go back to 1871 and a Swedish community in the Pennock, Minnesota, area. This was thirteen years before the meeting in Boone and fourteen years before the Evangelical Covenant denomination was formally organized. It was during the years of the Mission and Ansgar Synods (See *Search For Identity*). The congregations which were part of the Mission Synod became the nucleus for the Swedish Evangelical Free Church. The group at Pennock was torn by two controversies—affiliation with which synod and the question of having or not having membership for the local church.

As to which synod, the first pastor, J. G. Sjoquist, was a personal friend of Charles Anderson, a leader in the development of the Ansgar Synod. In spite of opposition by some who favored the Mission Synod, he pressured the congregation to join the Ansgar Synod in 1875. A long and often bitter struggle ensued. Sjoquist was followed by C. M. Youngquist, a leader in the other synod, who persuaded the group to withdraw from the Ansgar and join the Mission Synod in 1878. But this merely increased the dissension and by 1886 the church split into two congregations; the one is now the Salem Covenant Church of Pennock and the other the Evangelical Free Church of Kerkhoven. Eleven of the thirty-five members resigned when the congregation voted to become a member of the Covenant denomination. This was in 1886, shortly after the two denominations had been formed. The pastor of the Free Church, on its 35th anniversary, wrote that the friends met for five years without a formal organization (until 1891) and that the charter membership was 32. The Salem centennial publication (1971) contained the following: "Twenty-eight (of the 32) were at one time members of the Salem Church. How many others who are not listed in the minutes or who were not offficially members who worshipped at Salem who also withdrew in the controversy, we are not able to determine. It is sure, however, that the schism was a deep and painful one for all concerned and the whole community was affected."[38]

The other controversy was one in which the members of both churches were involved. It was common to so many of the early congregations—should the church have a membership list? Some believed, and expressed it strongly, that there should be no organized membership at all.

"The roll of the redeemed was written in the Lamb's Book of Life in Heaven, and therefore, any church membership roll was the work of the Devil."[39] The question was debated at a meeting on January 2, 1880. The minutes state that it was brought up at that time *again,* indicating it was not the first time. No decision was made. In October, 1882, the membership roll was abolished and a new method of enrollment considered. There was an added dimension to the problem since, when they first organized, there had been no rule restricting the membership to believers only. The minutes of the meeting on December 27, 1882 reported, "The enrollment question was settled by casting lots since no Scripture could be found which was definite." The lot cast was in favor of membership. Consequently, the candidates for membership would first have to meet with duly elected representatives authorized to examine and recommend them. The Salem Centennial book noted, "It may be an over-simplification to say the matter was settled. Strong opinions and feelings still persisted. Much credit, however, must be given this congregation and its leaders for the way they searched the Scriptures for the answers to their questions and applied a democratic process to govern and preserve the church."[40] By 1891, as far as the members who withdrew to form the Kerkhoven congregation were concerned, there seems to have been no controversy. The congregation had membership from its inception.

Some of the congregations who overcame opposition to membership rolls were possessed by another fear—that non-believers should slip into the membership and participate in the decision making process. An illustration of the extremes to which congregations went to protect against such is found in the story of the congregation at Phelps Center, Nebraska.

A mission meeting was announced for October 22, 1880.[41] Only four preachers responded, two of whom were laymen from the area. But Franson was in attendance and his presence along with the discussion on the teaching of the Scripture in the light of Christ's soon return resulted in "a downpour of God's grace," including a time of spiritual renewal for the believers and the "salvation of many souls." It also led to the organizing of the church. The report stated, "The people here have long limped on one foot and then on the other . . . but now they are getting strength in their legs. The overwhelming majority of them have long been thinking about the need for a local church structure according to the Bible, and now it is happening."

A complicated procedure was set up to insure a membership of believers only. The group first selected six of the brethren who were highly respected. They, in turn, nominated six others who were then approved by "the whole flock of those who confessed themselves Christian." The twelve followed the same procedure adding another six thereby bringing the charter membership to eighteen. Six were elected by the eighteen to serve as a membership committee. It presented six additional names which were accepted as members by the eighteen. This was repeated until the membership totaled thirty-two believers at which point the new congregation elected officers which would also serve as a standing committee on the admission and dismissal of members. By the time the report was published in the *Chicago Bladet* the membership had reached seventy.[42]

That the congregations organized by Franson during that

eventful ten-day period in 1880 seemed to have a common view regarding the constitution for the local church is revealed in the minutes of the organizing meeting at Keene on November 25, 1880. After electing Franson chairman of the meeting, opening devotions were conducted. Then three trustees and a secretary were chosen. Next a motion to name the new congregation, the Church of God in Keene, Kearney County, Nebraska, was passed followed by adjournment. However, there was a postscript to the minutes under the heading, Forgotten Business, which reported a second meeting on November 29 where the following motion was passed, "That the New Testament be the constitution of said church." This brings us back to the slogan of the revivals, "Where stands it written?" Thus, the Word of God would be not only the source of doctrine, the guide for life, the food for a growing faith, but provide the principles on which the business of the church was conducted.

The names chosen by the new congregations are interesting and also reveal a growing process since some of the names were changed several times including, of course, an eventual translation into English. While the Norwegian-Danish churches generally adopted the name Scandinavian Congregational Church, the first churches among those which would eventually form the Swedish Free Churches went by many and sometimes strange names. In addition to the Church of God there were the following: Swedish Free Mission, Swedish Evangelical Mission Congregation, Scandinavian Evangelical Free Mission Congregation, God's Congregation, Swedish Free Immanuel Church (at least three congregations used the name Immanuel—God with us—in the name), Scandinavian Free Mission Congregation, Swedish Christian Free Congregation, Christian Union Church, Swedish Christian Church, Evangelical Union Church. The First Evangelical Free Church of Minneapolis, for example, was known first as the Scandinavian Church of Christ (May 12, 1884). This was later changed to the First Evangelical Free Church (1926). The denomination was first called "Den Kristnas Gemensamma Verksamhet," translated in the fortieth anniversary booklet as The Christians' Confederated Activities.[43] The name was changed in 1896 to the Swedish Evangelical Free Mission. When incorporated in 1908 the name was again changed to the Swedish Evangelical Free Church of the United States of America. The name at that time was filed in English. In 1935, the name was changed to the Evangelical Free Church of America, which also became the name of the new denomination at the time of the merger in 1950.

The Norwegian-Danish, in addition to congregations known as Scandinavian Congregational Churches, most of which were changed to Evangelical Free Church by 1912, used a variety of other names including Norwegian Evangelical Free Church, Danish Evangelical Free Church, Scandinavian Evangelical Free Church, Norwegian-Danish Evangelical Free Church, Norwegian Evangelical Lutheran Church, Zion Evangelical Tabernacle, and Bloomington Temple. The name of the denomination was first the Norwegian-Danish Evangelical Free Church Association of North America. This was changed to the Norwegian-Danish Evangelical Free Church Association in 1925. Eventually, the "Norwegian-Danish" was also dropped.

FOOTNOTES—CHAPTER III

1. Broadbent, E. H., *The Pilgrim Church,* Fleming H. Revell Company, Westwood, N.J., 1955, p. 397.
2. *Golden Jubilee,* Swedish Evangelical Free Church of America, Minneapolis, MN, 1934, p. 16.
3. Ibid., p. 35
4. Ibid., p. 42
5. Carlsen, Nils C., *Liv og Virksomhet i Herrens Vingaard,* Evangelistens Forlag, Chicago, 1928, p. 123.
6. Olson, Arnold T., *The Search for Identity,* Free Church Press, Minneapolis, 1980, p. 71.
7. Walker, Williston, *The Creeds and Platforms of Congregationalism,* Pilgrim Press, Boston, 1893, p. 581.
8. *Golden Jubilee,* op. cit., p. 28.

9. Torjesen, Edv. from unpublished manuscript entitled, *Fredrik Franson and the Frontier Church.*
10. *Ibid.*
11. *Chicago Bladet,* October 8, 1880.
12. Carlsen, op. cit., pp. 226, 227.
13. Olson, Arnold T., *Believers Only,* Free Church Press, 1964.
14. Brolund, Erik, *Missions Vanarna: Jam Forelse,* Chicago, 1938, p. 110.
15. Daniels, W. H., *D. L. Moody and His Work,* American Press, Hartford, 1876, p. 104, 105.
16. Ibid., p. 105.
17. Ibid., p. 107.
18. Dexter, Henry M., *Congregationalism,* Noyes, Holmes and Company, Boston, 1874, p. 237-240.
19. Walker, op. cit., p. 108.
20. Carlsen, op. cit., p. 82.
21. Ibid., p. 157.
22. Ibid., p. 164.
23. Ibid., pp. 165, 166.
24. Ibid., pp. 195, 196.
25. Ibid., p. 123.
26. Ibid., pp. 135, 136.
27. Franson, Fredrik, *Prophesying Daughters,* translated from Swedish by Vernon Mortenson and Della E. Olson.
28. *Golden Jubilee,* op. cit., p. 35.
29. Ibid., p. 38.
30. *Chicago Bladet,* December 17, 1880.
31. Ibid.
32. Woodward, David B., *Aflame for God,* Moody Press, Chicago, 1966, pp. 54, 55.
33. *Chicago Bladet,* op. cit., December 17, 1880.
34. Woodward, op. cit., p. 55.
35. Ibid., p. 55.
36. Carlsen, op. cit., p. 158.
37. Ibid., p. 31.
38. *Crowning a Century,* Centennial Book published by Salem Covenant Church, Pennock, Minnesota, 1971.
39. Ibid., p. 15.
40. Ibid:, p. 15.
41. *Chicago Bladet.*
42. Ibid., December 10, 1980.
43. Modig, August H., *Ebenezer,* 1924, p. 7.

Chapter IV

THIS GRACE ALSO

𝕿herefore, as ye abound in every thing, in faith, and utterance, and knowledge, and in all diligence, and in your love to us, see that ye abound in this grace also. I speak not by commandment, but by occasion of the forwardness of others, and to prove the sincerity of your love.

(II Corinthians 8:7, 8)

*   *   *   *   *   *

And not that only, but who was also chosen of the churches to travel with us with this grace, which is administered by us to the glory of the same Lord, and declaration of your ready mind: Avoiding this, that no man should blame us in this abundance which is administered by us: Providing for honest things, not only in the sight of the Lord, but also in the sight of men.

(II Corinthians 8:19, 20, 21)

The pioneers, although enthusiastic for Christ and excited about the newly discovered power of faith, were a long way from maturity since one ingredient was missing. Several of the leaders have written about this. The experiences of Nils Carlsen were typical:

> They were united in the belief that the one who preaches the gospel should live of the gospel but they interpreted it to mean that the preacher and his family should be supported physically as well as spiritually through faith. Food, clothing, funds for travel should be obtained through faith in God. If friends were so moved, they could give funds voluntarily. There was no lack of emotion in the revivals but when the matter of an offering for the preacher came up, their hearts

were as hard as stone. They had not paid attention to the many places in God's Word which indicate that Paul received financial support and that he kept a record of what and from whom it was received . . . Now and then I received an offering; but in many cases it didn't even pay for my travel.[1]

On reaching the decision to give himself full-time to the work of evangelism, Carlsen sold his small general store, the proceeds from which kept him going for a very short time. When he came to a place he was welcomed by a few. On his departure, even following a time of revival, he heard, "Thanks for coming. Come again and God bless you." This was good, he thought, but would not provide for his family back home. It was easy to trust God when in his store filled with supplies, but now came the real tests of faith. There were times when he suffered from hunger, the cold weather, and lack of places to sleep—all in the midst of revival![2]

Itinerant evangelists had no fixed support. They were expected to simply trust the Lord. Local groups may have had a treasury but that was empty. The poor had nothing and those who had something were "stingy."[3] Many times there was not enough income to pay for a railroad ticket to the next town even at a half-fare clergy rate. So they walked, carrying their suitcases, and occasionally hitched a ride in a farmer's wagon for part of the way.

A. A. Anderson was another pioneer preacher active from the beginning of the Swedish Free Churches. He travelled as a home missionary and served for many years as superintendent of Missions for the Swedish Free Church. E. A. Halleen pays a wonderful tribute to Anderson in his autobiography: "We had among us men who were sweet and restful as a woodland meadow, characters that had by long experience and much affliction become mellow and tender. A. A. Anderson was a man of that type—a father to us younger men and a wise counsellor."[4]

His experiences were similar to those of Carlsen and many others. To him, the life of an itinerant evangelist was an experience of hatreds and hardships. Even in places where he was sincerely welcomed there were difficulties. He wrote of such a place:

Though my good hosts, with their sheepskin robes and heavy homespun clothing, did not seem to share my discomforts for me, with my light topcoat and felt hat, etc., the severe winter weather was indeed a trial. Often during the meetings I would bathe in sweat while my feet were like ice as the cold air streamed through the cracks between the shrunken floor planks which, of course, had been green when the houses were built. Then the chilling drafts from the open doors as the people departed and a bed with insufficient bedding all contributed to affect my health so that I suffered much from colic cramps. If the reader wonders why I did not buy suitable clothing, I can easily explain. The small reserve I had laid up from my wages was soon dissipated in traveling expenses, as the collections (the sole source of my income) were at that tme small at best and sometimes nil. Neither were the settlers in a position to share with me as they had only what was absolutely needed for their own well-being.[5]

Another example is the story of an experience in 1886:

It was in the month of December, shortly before Christmas, that we started on a journey to a certain place in Illinois, but decided to make a detour so as to reach a few other places where we desired an opportunity to preach. Difficulty arose because we were not known. The people we encountered evidently thought we had chosen an inopportune time to hold meetings, and therefore did not make us feel welcome. Then, too, the railroad company had charged us full fare when we had expected to travel on the usual half fare; and as no collection money was coming in to replenish our fast dwindling cash supply, we were in a predicament.

Something had to be done. But what? My cheerful companion, though of an adventurous spirit, now wore a doleful look. We wrote to friends in Chicago, advising them of our situation, and intended to wait for help from them. In order, therefore, to have enough money for lodging we decided to go without food. Supperless, we retired to a cheap hotel room and without breakfast the next morning we faced another cold winter day. There was no prospect of help until some time the following day. At this point the idea struck me that we might raise a little money by pawning our watches. This was done, but not until late in the day did we succeed in getting enough for our railway fare to our original destination. Having purchased the tickets we found that we had a few cents left over, and for this we bought a loaf of bread. Never did plain bread taste better or vanish more quickly.

We arrived at our destination early next morning, but no one was there to meet us as our friends did not know of our coming. We were strangers in this place also, and we found no one to direct us as we floundered along through the deep, new snow that early Sunday morning. Soon however, we found the street we were seeking, and our dear friends, who gave us a most hearty welcome. Our watches were immediately sent for and the discomforts of our journey were soon obliterated by the blessings we enjoyed in the series of meetings that followed.[6]

In another chapter of his autobiography he wrote of his days as Mission Superintendent:

There may at this time be a few questions that some of my friends would like to ask and that should here be answered. They might ask: "Who compensated you for your time and labor? How was your support maintained on these journeys?" My food as well as feed for my horses was generally given me without cost. I was also given small collections at different meeting places. In case of real necessity I had been granted the privilege of calling on our treasurer for a few dollars from the general fund. The greatest total for any single year that I had to call for was $65 and this seemed a huge sum. I believe this was the year I had to replace my worn-out buggy.

To the question: "How did you find your way?" which I have been asked many times, my answer is: that by frequent inquiry from travelers and others who were able to give authentic information, and by carefully observing landmarks, so as not to get my directions mixed, I had very little difficulty in this matter. Some have even asked me if I was not sometimes frightened as I lay out on the wild prairies at night. I must say that I have never been bothered with such fears but have always slept peacefully under my buggy after committing myself to the protection of the Almighty. The coyotes were my constant companions by day, and every night I was surrounded by them. Sometimes a gray wolf would make his appearance among them but would never offer to molest me. Neither did I try to harm them as I never carried any firearms. I did carry a hand ax but not to use as a weapon. I recall that once, however, I did get a scare when I found myself surrounded by a band of apparently hostile Indians.[7]

Since my own experience goes back over fifty years in the ministry, it also includes stories not unlike those of the pioneers. In 1928, while a student at the Free Church school, I went to Northern Minnesota for my first preaching mission. For a week's work I was given three silver dollars to be divided with the other young man with whom and in whose car I had made the trip. All the money went to him for gasoline. We stopped in a town about a third of the way back home where, unbeknown to me, my partner had purchased a car a few months earlier. He had hoped to receive enough of an offering to not only pay for gas and oil but for another payment on the car. The car was repossessed and we had to hitch a ride for the rest of the trip. Such an introduction to "full-time Christian service" was not exactly an encouragement to continue studies for the ministry. In the 1930s I traveled for a week with another pastor on a series of one night stands with both speaking each evening. We figured each message brought less than one dollar—maybe even that was in excess of their worth! However it did not cover our travel expenses.

One is apt to consider such reports as too subjective to provide a balanced account of the early experiences; but the *Golden Jubilee* book, written in 1930, supports them objectively as noted previously:

In the pioneer days the preachers furnished almost everything; sometimes even the lodging. No one was in fact responsible for them. They received what was given to them; nothing more. It was considered a privilege to preach the gospel, even if it had to be done gratis. The preachers, too, seemed to have favored this idea. Some of them ridiculed the idea of receiving a stipulated salary. A salaried minister was considered as belonging to the worldly denominations, and found little sympathy among our people. In most cases this position was taken in all sincerity; in other instances it was shrewdly planned.[8]

Out of his experience E. A. Halleen, who wrote the historical section of that book, was able to add an emotional dimension to the above observation:

Although brother Olson (Louis Olson—his associate in the early days) and I counted ourselves as belonging to the Free Church, yet strictly speaking we were free-lance itinerant preachers. No one had sent us out and no one was responsible for our support. And we chose that arrangement and made the best of it. And, believe me, the best was none too good. We lived from hand to mouth. Our shoes and clothing became worn and threadbare. As a rule friends noticed this but did nothing about it. Not all were that way. On our first visit to Minneapolis a kindhearted woman noticed my plight and gave me one dollar wherewith to purchase a new coat. However, I squandered the money on sinkers and coffee, and the coat remained unbought.

In the early years of my ministry there was a little Free Church in Oxford township, Isanti County, Minnesota. I visited this church off and on. Sometimes I would stay a week, ministering to the saints, and always without receiving any remuneration. On one of these visits I was with the friends over Thanksgiving and the following Sunday. For this I was to receive a liberal offering. And I needed the money. My shoes were worn so that I had to apply black ink wherever the white canvas became visible. Newspapers supplied me with inner soles.

Thanksgiving Day came. A Thanksgiving sermon was delivered. The reader may not believe it, but a good spirit was felt in the meeting. The chairman of the church, who was also my host, after making an earnest plea in my behalf, took his own hat and proceeded to collect the Thanksgiving offering. In due time he returned to the platform and showed me the hat—it was empty.

We closed the service in the usual manner, and I continued to minister to the friends over the following Sunday. Happily I still had some ink. That, and a determination to press on and not to give up. The pioneer days were eventful enough, but much less remunerative. But somehow similar experiences leave valuable ingredients in the bottom of the glass. And—something to talk about later.

I shall never forget the emotions depicted in the face of the brother who that day won for himself the distinction of having taken the smallest Thanksgiving offering ever known. The dear brother was as surprised as I was; and as penniless. Perhaps the others were as destitute.

Driving home from church that day my brother was very talkative. Some folks enjoy talking, but he was not that kind. Some talk everlastingly. Some talk to hide the fact that they are not thinking; others to hide their thoughts. Not a few talk because they can't think. I believe the brother talked to hide his chagrin over the result of the meeting. Maybe. Strangely enough, I never returned to that place. Not because of the small offering, but because the work died out. The church building was moved to another place, but even there it failed.[9]

It wasn't only the matter of funds for travel and support for one's family. There was also the problem of lodging for the night while on the road, as Anderson indicated. The pioneers often slept in the open. Like Jesus, they had no place to lay the head. Halleen wrote of having to sleep one night in a cemetery:

What the pioneers wanted was life and life more abundant; that and a genuine passion for souls, which would prove itself by being adventurous and self-sacrificing. What a challenge! There has been nothing like it. Never. Very few of the pioneer preachers could afford a horse. And oftentimes the farmers found no time to take the preacher from one place to another. He had, therefore, to be prepared to walk, carrying his belongings. If the collections received were fairly liberal, he could travel at least part way by train. But travel he must. And there was romance amidst the hardships.

Having held three services one day in a certain place we were offered no entertainment for the night. For that I have been grateful many a time. It happened to be at such time of the year and on such a night that could be called a night of nights. We became actually enthralled as we stood outside the church alone viewing the stellar glories. That and the feeling of a day well spent. True, it had been a strenuous day, and more strenuous to get to the place. But all that was easily forgotten in the adventure.

* * * * * *

The resting place of the dead was to be our Bethel for the night. And what a splendid opportunity was afforded us to enjoy the glories of the night! Occasionally a farmer's dog could be heard in the distant farmyard, or the tinkling of bells in the fields, or the doleful call of animals to their mates. Above us the starry firmament was visible while soft breezes brought a refreshing calmness to the soul. It was a balmy summer night. The grass was soft and sweet between the mounds. Sleep was likewise sweet.[10]

Lest we judge the people of that period too severly, we would be amiss if we did not explain some of the factors contributing to the early lack of an understanding of Biblical stewardship. First, we must not forget that the early believers were immigrants out of the State Churches of the Scandinavian countries. In the old country the citizens were taxed to finance the church and support the clergy. The only offerings were the annual, often compulsory Christmas gift to the priest and the school teacher. The idea of offerings for preachers was foreign and, in some cases, even offensive to them. The itinerant Free Church preachers usually came to the Scandinavian communities uninvited. As Halleen noted, "Strictly speaking, we were free-lance, itinerant preachers. No one had sent us out and no one was responsible for our support."

Further, there wasn't much of what we call cash flow among the people in the rural areas. Much of the business was carried on in the form of barter. For example, the farmer's wife brought eggs to the store in exchange for sugar and salt. The farmer would exchange grain for goods. Even an appeal for needy saints in another village would fall on unreceptive ears when their own needs were just as great. There was also the matter of debts, as many immigrants had borrowed money to come to America. The new land with "gold and silver on the trees" would make it possible to repay their benefactors in a short time. Since they were mistaken there followed the slow process of repaying the debts which took all the cash they could spare. Not all borrowed money. Some were saving money to send for others. My father's oldest brother came over first and when he had saved enough he sent passage money for the second brother and the two of them eventually sent funds for the third. My father-in-law came over and earned and saved enough to send for his wife and four children.

Finally, there was the matter of priorities. The converts were occupied with newly found joy in their experience of salvation. Stewardship was far down on the list as they did what Paul mentions at the beginning of this chapter—learning to exercise faith and express that faith in words. They were also gaining in "knowledge, enthusiasm," and the "love for the teachers." But they were slow in adding "generosity to their virtues."[11]

Once this was done, there was no stopping them. Carlsen, who wrote of the early believers having "hearts of stone" when it came to generosity, lived long enough to see the change. He wrote in 1928, "Although there is no prescribed rule within the Evangelical Free Church regarding offerings to the cause of Christ, many of the brothers and sisters tithe while others follow the practice of laying aside what they can to bring to the church on the first day of the week."[12]

Generosity began with the support of missions overseas. Again quoting Carlsen, "When it comes to overseas missions, I doubt there is a denomination, which in comparison to its size, contributes as much money and sends forth as many missionaries as do the Evangelical Free Churches."[13]

Much of this interest in giving was due to the influence of Fredrik Franson. Once he caught the vision he was able with the help of the Holy Spirit to transmit the same vision and passion to others. Missions came first. This was true in both of the denominations prior to the merger and has continued to have top priority. The idea of funds to train workers, except for missionaries, adequate support for pastors, etc., developed much more slowly. My predecessor in the president's office told of a letter, accompanying a generous donation, giving instruction that the money was for the support of missions overseas which concluded, "We want every penny of this gift to go to the *Lord's work* and not a penny to Headquarters." Even today it is much easier to raise money for work across the sea than for work across the street. Home Missions struggles with deficits while Overseas enjoys its balanced budgets. No one would suggest a greater support for education, evangelism and extension at the expense of missions overseas but many are searching for ways to bring the generosity for these equally important causes up to the same level. It was the fish caught by Peter at the command of Jesus that had the coin in its mouth! The expansion of the work at home would make for further advances across the sea. In its stumbling toward maturity the church has been slowed because one leg has been shorter than the other. The limp, though still noticeable, is much less so.

We must not, however, overlook the progress made in all phases of stewardship. It is that progress which will be reviewed in the rest of the chapter. Each step, interestingly, has been in the direction of a well-balanced program for work at home and abroad. The Evangelical Free Church has come a long way. Omitted will be one of the greatest stories of all; namely, education for Christian service which is left to a separate volume. The same is true of the growth in stewardship for missions overseas.[14] It will be necessary to review the development of stewardship in three parts—(1) the former Swedish Evangelical Free Church, (2) the former Norwegian-Danish Evangelical Free Church Association, (3) the merged Evangelical Free Church of America from 1950 to 1980. This will not be an analysis of income but a report on the funds which were set up to meet specific needs and thus going beyond support resulting from a current appeal; the support of missionaries at home and abroad, and personalized as it still is today and properly so in the Free Church structure.

The first recommendation to set up a special fund in the Swedish Free Church was made at the conference in 1917. Though referred to as a pension fund it developed into the Preachers' Help Fund and later the Free Church Help Society. The rules were adopted in 1918.[15] The purpose of the fund was to help needy, sick or retired pastors, and the widows and children of deceased pastors. Income, in addition to investments, was to come from a small annual contribution by each pastor, an annual offering from each church, and a dollar donation from each member of the Ministerial as a memorial upon the death of a fellow pastor. The fund really was not a success. Seldom was the balance over $3,000 at the end of a fiscal year and the most ever disbursed in a year was $1,000. Either it was a fund before its time or the pastors were too modest to push for the annual offering in the churches they served.

An editorial in the *Beacon* in 1944 was headlined, *A Pension Plan at Last!* It stated:

> By an overwhelming majority of votes, the sixtieth annual conference adopted the annuity and aid plan—a plan that aims to give more substantial aid to our older and needy ministers, as well as death benefits to beneficiaries or lump sums or monthly payments to participants on reaching the age of 65 years. The younger ministers will pay $25 a year into the fund and the churches will be urged to give an equivalent of $1 per member per year. Eighty percent of the offerings or bequests will be prorated to the credit of the members and twenty percent distributed among older and needy ministers.[16]

It's interesting that the driving force behind the adoption of this plan was a missionary—Arthur Lindquist. He had worked hard and long rounding up support for its adoption. Like the disciples who were called upon to pray the Lord of the harvest to send forth laborers only to become the "sent ones" themselves, Lindquist was called upon to travel in the interest of the fund. His task then became one of convincing local congregations to implement the plan.

The minutes indicate that there was a good deal of discussion at the annual meeting over adoption of the plan and the editorial notes that "an overwhelming majority" approved it. This would indicate that it was not unanimous. Could it be that some of the old attitude still remained? One of the older pastors objected to the $25 annual fee although he was well beyond the age when he would have to pay. He also felt it was interfering with a pastor's private life. His experience in the early years had left permanent scars. He had been a partner of Nils Carlsen in those difficult years when all they received was a "thank you." He was a brother dearly loved to whom $25 was a year's income when he started out preaching. However, the plan was well received by the churches.

The second venture was the adoption of the $50,000 program for a revolving fund called The Home Missions Extension Fund to aid new and small churches through loans at a low interest for building projects. This was adopted by the General Conference in 1945. President Halleen wrote an explanation of the program which is also applicable to the Revolving Fund following the merger:

> This fund will meet a great need in our work. So many small churches and groups are in need of just that kind of help. They need to build or to renovate, or perhaps to move their church building to a more advantageous location, but lack the necessary funds, at least for the time being. And church loans are frowned upon by banks and loan companies; and if loans are granted the interest rate is high. Especially is this true where the groups are small and in most need of a loan. It is natural that these groups should turn to headquarters for help. But so far very little help has been rendered for the simple reason that we have had very little money assigned for such a purpose.

> With the inauguration of the Extension Fund it will be possible to assist more places and groups with loans at a low rate of interest. The payment of these loans plus the accrued interest

will revolve back to the fund, thereby keeping the fund intact for the purpose for which it was started. It is also expected that donations will be made from time to time to this fund, thereby strengthening this phase of our work. It is understood, or should be, that these loans will be handled through our District Conferences and underwritten by their officers.

In granting these loans our home base will be strengthened and enabled to do more effective work locally. It will also enable otherwise weak groups to do more direct missionary work, both on home fields and foreign. Better church buildings and facilities will in turn attract more attention as well as interest from the outside, which will enlarge the attendance at Sunday School and preaching services. It will also have an awakening and wholesome effect upon the children and youth of the church and community. The spiritual home should keep step with the individual home, to say the least.[17]

The Women's Missionary Society assumed the responsibility for providing $25,000 of the fund as a three-year project which it completed in two years.

As far back as 1925 the denomination launched an annuity program, offering what were called annuity bonds. The first one was purchased by Hannah V. Peterson with half of its remainder value designated for the Children's Home at Holdrege, Nebraska, and the other half to the rest of the work of the denomination. The plan was never really promoted as it could have been, for by the time of the merger in 1950, twenty-five years after it had been launched, there was only $26,802 in the account. The potential of such a plan could have been far reaching. The Norwegian-Danish Association had none, although many of the members were looking for such a program. As a result, many dollars which would have come to the Free Church work went to other organizations which had such a plan simply because the Free Church was so slow in recognizing the possibilities.

Carlsen wrote of an experience in Kansas (1891) which reveals how little some of the pioneer leaders knew about such matters:

One day my host asked how he might support missionary work after his death. At first I thought he was joking, although I knew him well enough to know that he wasn't of the joking kind. I said, "Isn't it enough that you support the Lord's work while you are alive without continuing to do it after you are dead?" He replied, "You know we have no children and all of our possessions have come to us from the hand of God. None of our relatives are Christians and when they come to visit us it is only for the obvious purpose of keeping up a connection. They are hoping to be the beneficiaries of our estate upon our death. But what we have is loaned to us by God. We are but His stewards. Therefore, I want to return it to Him. There are many who want the estate but will squander it in a short time. However, my desire is that it might remain and serve God until Jesus comes." I had to reply that I didn't know how it could be done. Today (1928) I could tell him how it can be done but now the brother has most likely left to be with Jesus.[18]

One can forgive Carlsen. He was no different from many other leaders at that time, but the inability to assist this generous brother was a disservice to him and to the cause of Christ. May it never happen again!

We digress to share another story about this man. During his meetings, Carlsen would hitch up his wagon early in the afternoon to pick up people for the evening services. When the time came for the offering, he would give far in excess of the others assembled but did so in small change as an encouragement to the rest. There would be no flaunting of his wealth or generosity. "He did not want it to appear that only he had given. He would rather have it appear that five or ten others had also done so."[19]

The Norwegian-Danish Evangelical Free Church Association launched its first major fund drive in 1918. It began as an idea in the mind and on the heart of Krag P. Wuflestad in North Dakota. He suggested to Carlsen that a Mission Aid and Loan Fund of $50,000 be established through a ten-year pledge program. This would be used for loans to churches at low interest for building projects. At the annual meeting in 1918 the goal was increased to $100,000. The faith, or perhaps it was emotion mixed with unrealism, had gone from little to much, so at the conference in 1919 the goal was increased once more, this time to $200,000 with the first half reserved for the Loan Fund and the second half to be used to meet special needs. Carlsen was asked to travel in the interest of this fund which he did until 1924. Carlsen insisted he was asked only after others turned the assignment down and that he was the least qualified for the task. "Not so," wrote the editor of Evangelisten following Carlsen's death:

> Carlsen was a capable revivalist—and an instrument to the salvation of many souls both in America and in his native Denmark. But this willing servant was also used in other ministries. When the Evangelical Free Church decided to establish the Mission Aid and Loan Fund he was chosen as the most suited to head up the ingathering. He did it to everyone's satisfaction. It was a very difficult assignment but he carried it out with such tact, persuasiveness, and effort that he gained many new friends. The work of the Free Church profited and was strengthened by his sacrificial service.[20]

Apparently, Carlsen approached the task with the same enthusiasm and fearlessness in convincing potential donors that he used in approaching people regarding the acceptance of Christ as Savior. His method was "eyeball to eyeball," similar to the one used in the Jubilee Fund drive 1957-1959. By 1923 the assets of the fund had almost reached the first goal of $100,000 ($96,286.59). In 1924, a representative from North Dakota requested that the conference agree to reduce the amounts remaining on the personal commitments to half the balance because of the difficult economic conditions. The effects of the drought and grasshopper plague would last a long time. It must be noted to the credit of the people that they were not ignoring their pledges. To them, these were obligations to be paid in full unless the denomination released them from part of the obligation. This is a characteristic of Free Church members. History gives evidence that their pledges are as good as cash. During my time in the president's office I received payment of a pledge made to this fund fifty years earlier! By granting the request to reduce the balance on the pledges, the assets of the fund were also reduced so that by the next year it was down to $42,000.

The Fund suffered in two other ways. The denominational paper and the school were continually experiencing deficits and, since the Fund was the only source of cash, much was loaned to the two institutions, leaving little for loans to churches. This discouraged those who had made pledges. The final blow, and a devastating one it was, came when much of the cash was lost as a result of an unwise investment. By the time of the merger in 1950, the assets had dwindled to less than $20,000. Many who still owed some in their pledges simply lost confidence in the leadership.

There was a difference in Carlsen's approach and those who raised the funds in the Swedish Free Church. The latter was done more or less through appeals to the churches, while Carlsen called on individuals. His experience provided a wealth of stories, some of which bear repeating. As in personal witnessing the response ranged from receptiveness to rage.

In introducing the account of his experiences, Carlsen stated an awareness of the difficulties he faced in his new assignment: "I have learned from experience that one often meets believers who will shout hallelujah so loudly at the meetings that one can barely hear his own voice but who hurriedly leave when one asks for a dollar for the work." After the drive was over he wrote that the ingathering for the loan fund was, in many ways, a trial. He claimed that some experiences had been blessed while a few were not.[21]

One young man with limited income designated $300 as his ten-year pledge. Carlsen assumed it was an error and that he had meant $30. But the young man had not made a mistake. Another pledged $1,000. Carlsen, knowing he made only $70 to $80 a month, thought he had meant $100 so called him to verify the pledge and was informed that he knew what he was doing and that the pledge was a matter between him and God!

One laborer with limited income and a large family fought a battle with himself. He was so anxious to make a pledge. One voice said, "You need the money for yourself and yours. You are poor. Others are not giving so much." Another voice whispered, "Give in faith. It is better to give the money than use it for extremely fashionable dresses for your daughters so that they might look like women of the theater or half naked prostitutes who would bring disgrace to the believing parents." He pledged $250 and was joined by a fourteen-year-old daughter and a nine-year-old son who pledged $100 and $50 respectively. A thirteen-year-old signed one pledge for $50 and another for $75. Not wishing to embarrass the boy, Carlsen spoke to his father. The father smiled and said, "Is it not better that my son gives money to the fund than to squander it on tobacco and the like which destroy both body and soul? I shall see to it that the lad is able to pay his pledge."[22]

Carlsen, we must remember, is the man who encountered the stinginess of people twenty to thirty years earlier. He had difficulty in recognizing the change.

These stories represent only one side of the record. When Carlsen called on one of the wealthier men in a community asking if he would be willing to make a pledge, the man complained that he was in the process of electrifying his farm and so could not donate to the fund. Carlsen called again a few days later to ascertain if he had changed his mind. The answer was no. "Not even ten dollars a year? . . . or five?" The answer was again negative. Carlsen noticed he had eight horses, fifteen cattle, several calves, so he said, "God can bless these animals for you so that they might bring you more. How about $2.50 a year?" The answer was again a no. Persistency was not one of Carlsen's weaker traits!

He called on another who replied that he didn't believe in giving money to old preachers. (Carlsen was seventy at that time.) Carlsen insisted it was not a fund for preachers, assuring him, sarcastically, that they would keep the preachers on a diet of air and cold water. That didn't help either!

In spite of a few disappointments, Carlsen, who called himself a "stubborn Dane," continued and succeeded. He felt the ingathering would have been a greater success if it had been handled by a better man; but he believed the money would be a great blessing to coming generations if it was administered properly. It hurts to remember that he lived to see the deterioration of the Fund. What a heartbreak it must have been. Just one final note on this remarkable man whom I met and heard often as a lad and young minister. His autobiography was published in 1928. He died in 1932 at the age of 80. The years between 1928 and 1932 were spent in the area of Detroit Lakes, Minnesota, cutting and selling firewood to pay up the debt incurred in publishing the book!

Several books have been written about the life and work of Fredrik Franson, while Nils Carlsen's work has gone unnoticed since nothing has been written about him in the English language. His role in the Norwegian-Danish Evangelical Free Church Association and also in several of the Swedish congregations is remarkable. Here was a man with no church background whatever and no theological training. In fact, he hadn't even had the simplest of Bible teaching such as most children have experienced in Sunday School. During his early days as a revivalist, recorded in the preceding chapter, he was anti-establishment. Yet, he became an outstanding teacher of the Word of God and a leading churchman. He was a great student, a fast learner, and a flexible man willing to learn and adopt new ideas regarding the church. He was also the Paul to many Timothys. A number of pastors, some of whom became denominational leaders, had their field training under his tutelage. Among these were H. A. C. Anderson, T. J. Fransen, A. Handy, Anders Herje, Albert Lunde (he became one of Norway's greatest revivalists), Johannes Lunde, Torlief Lunde, John Nelsen, N. W. Nelsen, Tom Olson, Hans Sande, Ole Sande, Oscar Walstad and Alfred Wold.

Prior to his conversion, Carlsen served Satan wholeheartedly. When he became a Christian, he served His Lord wholeheartedly. He paid little attention to what might have been an easier way or to what might have been self-serving. He made many sacrifices. His family was often in difficult circumstances financially. He often sat all night in a railroad station, sometimes because of having no money for a hotel and at other times to save the little he had to get to the next place for meetings.

It was said at his memorial on August 23, 1932, that he was original in so many ways. This was especially true in his preaching and in the strange combination of languages he used. He had little tolerance for those who used the sermon outlines of others. One could not easily determine if his language was Danish, Norwegian, Swedish, English or something else—he called it Scandinavian. People listened and understood him which was the most important. As a lad, I heard him many times and was fascinated by his speech. Later, as a seminary student, I forgot the language as I was entranced by the unique and original way in which he developed his message from a passage of Scripture. I made a mistake on one occasion. Anxious to show respect for this man of God, I took his heavy, furlined coat off from the rack and offered to help him put it on. He grabbed it and said, "I am not that old yet." He was seventy-eight at the time.

One of his colleagues who was present during the final days of his life wrote of it later: "The work of the Free Church was the burden of his heart to the end. He prayed for its people, its congregations, and its preachers to the very end. On Saturday, the day before he died, he gathered all his children around his bedside and bade them farewell. He seemed suddenly to have received supernatural strength in spite of his frailty. He called each by name, held their hands in his, talked and prayed for each individually and then invoked God's blessing upon them and on the rest of us who were present. It was one of the most holy moments in my experience."[23]

In the book, *The Search for Identity*, there is a chapter entitled, "There Were Giants in the Earth." Although Carlsen was not one of the founders of the denomination, he must be included among the giants in the history of the two denominations, both of which were represented at the memorial service. In addition to serving Christ and the Church in soliciting funds for the Mission Aid and Loan Fund, he served on the School Board and the Board of the Western District and traveled as the field representative for the denomination.

The second project in the Norwegian-Danish Association was a pension fund for ministers known as the Ministerial Pension Fund, introduced and approved in 1926. Its stated purpose was to assist retired or ill pastors and widows of pastors. The plan was to be financed by an annual donation of $10 from each pastor and a yearly offering from the congregations as well as special gifts and legacies.[24] It was slow in developing as C. T. Dyrness reported the following year. One reason, he declared, was that the pastors were too "egotistical" to promote the plan. Nevertheless it kept growing and was active, or one might better say survived, until the time of the merger. As mentioned earlier, the school and the Publishing Society were always in financial difficulty. The latter was called the "bottomless pit." At one conference it was decided to again borrow from the Ministerial Pension Fund to save the Publishing Society from bankruptcy. The treasurer, a strong willed general contractor, refused to carry out the decision claiming, in view of history, it could not be repaid. He insisted that the fund was independent of the denomination in its administration and could not be touched by the "whims of conference delegates or cries from the departments for help."

He would not even surrender the balance on hand to a new treasurer lest it eventually wind up as a loan to the work. Finally, some years after I was elected to the Pension Board, he invited me to lunch at which time he said, "I trust you (for which I thanked him) and don't believe you would permit the money which is on reserve for our ministers to be squandered. After lunch, I want you to go with me to the bank and I'll get a cashier's check for the entire balance in the account." Whether he was right or wrong, and in his heart he was never wrong, the fund was saved. Several of the pastors were privately thankful for the brother's stubborness.

The believers in both denominations had come a long way from the 1880s to 1950. Their spirit of generosity was catching up to their expressions of faith and their "knowledge, enthusiasm, and love . . . " The new generation, not influenced by the practices of the State Churches in Scandinavia, helped, but it alone could not have brought about a change without the transformation of attitude towards Christian stewardship by the pioneers. May we ever be thankful.

But there were more steps to take in the move towards maturity following the merger. Support of all phases of the work has increased to the extent that the Evangelical Free Church has for several years ranked among the top five of all the denominations in per capita giving to the work in general and to missions in particular. What follows is a brief review of the Revolving and Pension Funds, the Jubilee Fund, Shareholders, and Christian Investors Foundation.

The Mission Aid and Loan Fund of the Norwegian-Danish Evangelical Free Church Association and the Revolving Extension Fund of the Swedish Evangelical Free Church were merged into one known as the Revolving Fund. It continues to provide loans at very low interest to young congregations for building programs.

The two pension funds, similar in their operations, were

also merged. In 1971 this plan was upgraded to what is now one of the best retirement plans among all the denominations in America. It is known as the Free Church Ministers and Missionaries Retirement Plan.

In 1954 a program known as Shareholders was launched which would provide grants in cash for church buildings to new congregations. Each person signing up for the program agrees to donate, upon notice, a minimum of a specified gift. It began as a one dollar share with no more than two projects a year. This was gradually increased both as to frequency and amount for each. There are now twelve projects per year (1980) and the minumum amount for each is $2.50. During the first twenty-five years of the Fund's existence, 120 congregations were aided in this manner.

A new and separate corporation was formed in 1959 known as the Christian Investors Foundation. This is a plan in which Free Church people invest (not donate) money at a rate of interest comparable to that paid by banks. The funds are then loaned to churches and other institutions at a rate of interest sufficient to pay the investors interest promised them and to cover the cost of administration. The loans are secured by first mortgages available, as funds permit, to organizations which qualify. The first paragraphs of the Articles of Incorporation clearly state the purpose of the foundation:

(1) The establishment, support, benefit, extension and financial aid of the congregations of The Evangelical Free Church of America, allied and cooperating for the advancement of Christian faith and life in conformity to the teachings of the Holy Bible through Christian instruction and Christian missions in this and foreign countries, whereby any or all the needs of such congregations may be provided, including, but not by way of restriction, churches, chapels, parsonages, seminaries, schools, camps, assemblies and other similar institutions and the furnishing, equipping, maintenance and operation of the same;

(2) The establishment, support, benefit, extension and finan-

cial aid of hospitals, convalescent homes, homes for the aged, nursing homes, lying-in institutions, dispensaries, medical missions, societies for the provision of surgical or medical aid or appliances, institutions for the rest, relief or cure of sick or crippled persons;

(3) The support, benefit, extension and financial aid of nursing and also the practice of the professions of medicine and nursing by duly licensed practitioners thereof and of the development and improvement of the techniques, methods, procedures and administration in connection with any of the foregoing institutions and of studies and teaching in those fields.

A Department of Stewardship, long overdue, was established in 1966. While the Swedish Free Church inaugurated an Annuity plan as early as 1925, it never reached its potential. The department, staffed by people trained in deferred giving—Annuities, Charitable Remainder Trusts, Charitable Remainder Unitrusts, Revocable Trust Agreements, Flexible Gifts, Deferred Payment Gift Annuity, Gifts of Life Insurance, homes and farms with life estate residency rights for donor, wills, etc. is one of the fastest growing in the Free Church organization.

It can certainly be said that in spite of its stumbling a century ago the Church has moved, step-by-step, toward adding "generosity to the virtues."

The best and most inspiring evidence of this is the story of the Diamond Jubilee Fund part of a three-year Program for Progress culminating in the seventy-fifth anniversary of the denomination in 1959 which is so important that it bears sharing in some detail, for it was through that drive that the members of the local churches—the grass roots—came face to face with "where stands it written" and responded to the teachings of the Scriptures on stewardship.

The program started off with a goal of $300,000 as part of a three-year Program for Progress scheduled to culminate at the 75th anniversary of the denomination in 1959. The goal was raised to $800,000 and then to $2,500,000. When completed the results were in excess of $2,700,000!

The Program for Progress was much more than a drive for money. Had it been merely a fund drive, one might not have witnessed such results. The goals as adopted in 1956 were:

1. A deepening of our spiritual life.
2. A development and extension of all the tangible facilities which increase our effectiveness in spreading the Gospel.
3. A great impact for Christ on our community, nation and world.

Certain objectives were set, apart from the goal for funds:

75 new congregations added to our fellowship by 1959.
7500 new members.
75 new missionaries.
75 new students for our Seminary
7500 new subscribers to our official publication.
75 new Sunday Schools, youth groups, and women's missionary societies.
2 new mission fields abroad.
2 new district organizations.

Every one of the goals was reached—a fact overlooked by some in their enthusiasm about the results of the Jubilee Fund. The money from the Jubilee Fund was to be used for captial investments and improvements. Of the $800,000, half was to be kept in the local congregations for building projects. The local projects included new church buildings, Sunday School additions, remodeling of existing buildings, parsonages, additional land for building and parking, redecoration of church buildings, new heating systems, additional Sunday School equipment, organs, branch churches, payment on expansion programs already in progress or completed, etc. The other half was to be divided as follows:

Trinity debt	$ 75,000
Education expansion	75,000
Home and foreign missions expansion	75,000

Headquarters building debt	75,000
Revolving Fund	100,000
	$400,000

Once the goal was raised to two and one-half million, additions to the above mentioned projects were made, providing more funds for the erection of buildings for what was then called Trinity Seminary and Bible College. Eventually the site was changed to Bannockburn, Illinois, and the Fund made it possible to pay cash for the land. The cost of the first 35 acres was $146,000. The remaining 44 acres were donated.

During the years of the Program for Progress other developments were taking place, the most far reaching of which was the decision to start a junior college in Western Canada. This called for a change in the anticipated distribution of the Fund. Money from the churches in Canada designated for Trinity in Illinois would go to the school in British Columbia.

As for the plan itself, it was to be a person-to-person appeal. Evangelical Free Church pastors were used in solicitation following an opening banquet in each church. We sought to follow the pattern for stewardship laid down in the Scriptures. In doing so we also ignored what has been called "the mossiest myths of fund raising"—that mere publicity can raise substantial sums of money and that another easy way to raise money is by some simple application of the multiplication table. For example, persuading one hundred donors to pledge $1,000 each would augment to $100,000. Or, by persuading a predetermined number to give $1,000 each, and a larger number, $500, and an even larger number to give $250, etc., a goal could be reached. Rather, the Scriptural basis for stewardship was presented at each banquet and also in the *Evangelical Beacon*. It is repeated here for future reference.

I. *The giving is to be by the individual.* "Every man according as he purposeth in his heart, so let him give; not grudgingly, or of necessity: for God loveth a cheerful giver" (II Cor. 9:7). It is because of this instruction that we do not ask the church to set aside a sum out of its budget but rather that we be permitted to appeal to each member individually. We do not believe that a pastor or board of trustees has a right to decide on behalf of its people whether or not they can afford to give more than they are doing or whether or not they wish to participate.

II. *The giving is to be on a weekly basis.* "On the first day of the week let every one of you lay by him in store . . . " (I Cor. 16:2). Note that again reference is made to the individual. Because of the instruction to lay aside on a weekly basis, we are not seeking large outright gifts although they are welcome and gladly accepted. The plan, however, seeks to encourage people to lay aside a little extra each week for a period of three years. It is possible to write out a check to the local church at the beginning of the year or to the Jubilee Fund at the beginning of the three-year period and then immediately forget the work. But with the individual's weekly donation goes his weekly concern, interest, and prayer. We seek that above all else.

III. *The giving is to be proportionate.* "Let every one of you lay by him in store, as God has prospered him" (I Cor. 16:2). Note again the emphasis on the individual. It is not as God has prospered the church. It is because of this instruction that we are careful not to set goals for churches. Churches which do so are not following the suggestions of the Commission. No local goals are set. We are simply asking for an opportunity to make an appeal and are willing to accept whatever the individuals are able to pledge. For this reason, we are speaking constantly in terms of projects rather than dollars and cents. It is true that definite sums are to be allocated to certain projects but the program is not set up on a "so much per member or so much per church" basis.

IV. *The giving is to be on a pledge basis.* The Bible speaks of both the pledge and the performance. "And herein I give my advice: for this is expedient for you, who have begun before, not only to do, but also to be forward a year ago. Now therefore perform the doing of it; that as there was a readiness to will, so there may be a performance also out of that which ye have" (II Cor. 8: 10, 11). These instructions were regarding money promised by the people of the church at Corinth for famine relief in Jerusalem. Making a pledge is an act of faith. To give what one already has takes no faith, but to promise money that one does not even possess yet is an expression of faith. That is why the pledge cards use the word "covenant" rather than "pledge." It is an agreement with God by which the believer will give as God provides the health and means. The cards are not binding as legal documents and state that the promise may be changed by notifying the treasurer in writing. Thus it is an agreement with God rather than the church.

V. *The administration of the appeal is handled by someone appointed specifically for that purpose.* "We have sent with him the brother, whose praise is in the gospel throughout all the churches; and not that only but who was chosen of the churches to travel with us with this grace, which is administered by us to the glory of the same Lord, and declaration of your ready mind . . . " (II Cor. 8:18, 19). The reader should study the entire chapter. The grace referred to here is the grace of giving especially as it relates to the funds collected for the above mentioned project. God has given many gifts to the church and among these the gifts of administration. People have been slow to recognize this point. We bring in the evangelist from outside the church in an effort to win souls to Christ. We bring in the Bible teacher from outside the church to lead our people into the deeper things of God. We believe these laborers are worthy of their hire and do not hesitate to provide money for transportation, lodging, and an honorarium besides.

Yet, some oppose the bringing in of an administrator from outside the local church to lead the people in stewardship and protest the use of a single penny to meet the cost of such an emphasis. This we do in spite of the fact that the Word of God is more explicit in its instructions for the calling of a man to assist in the raising and administration of money than it is in the instructions for an evangelistic campaign or a Bible conference.

VI. *The giving is administered by men responsible to the people of the churches.* "Avoiding this, that no man should blame us in this abundance which is administered by us, providing for honest things, not only in the sight of the Lord, but in the sight of men" (II Cor. 8:20, 21). Not only do our people have a voice in the distribution of the Jubilee Fund in the local church but throughout the denomination by way of the delegates to the general conference. Further, those from the denomination who assist the local church in the stewardship program bring with them suggestions for keeping records. Furthermore, any church participating in the Jubilee program is entitled to counsel, without cost, for a period of three years in the matters of church finances by those who are gifted and experienced in this area of church work. Every penny will be accounted for.

We do not believe that Christians ought to give any of their tithe to individuals or organizations which fail to reveal exactly how such money is used. In the Program for Progress, as in all funds handled by the Evangelical Free Church of America, we go even further than that. The people control the administration of the money. Audited financial reports are presented to the conference, budgets for the coming year are prepared and approved by the same conference. It is not enough to provide "things honest in the sight of the Lord" and proceed on the assumption that as long as the Lord knows, no one else is entitled to information. The Bible says that those handling the funds must also provide for things honest "in the sight of men."

VII. *The giving according to this pattern is Christ-like.* "I speak not by commandment, but by the occasion of the forwardness of others, and to prove the sincerity of your love. For ye know the grace of our Lord Jesus Christ, that, though he was rich, yet for your sakes he became poor, that ye through his poverty might be rich" (II Cor. 8:8,9). Christ not only had more to say on the subject of stewardship than any other topic but the giving of Himself is used in this chapter as a reason why we should give of our money to the Lord's work. We have no right to take this verse out of its setting.

VIII. *Giving is recognized as a spiritual matter.* "Moreover, brethren, we do you to wit of the grace of God bestowed on the churches of Macedonia; how that in great trial of affliction and abundance of their joy and their deep poverty abounded unto the riches of their liberality. For to their power, I bear record, yea, beyond their power they are willing of themselves; praying us with much entreaty that we should receive the gift, and take upon us the fellowship of ministering to the saints. And this they did, not as we had hoped (or beyond our expectations), but first gave their own selves to the Lord, and unto us by the will of God" (II Cor. 8:1-5). Dedication to God preceded the program of stewardship. We sincerely believe we have endeavored to follow this plan. The year 1957 has been a year of evangelism. It began in January with an emphasis on personal consecration, then lessons in soul winning, followed by the various types of evangelism. This has brought great blessing to the churches which followed the program.

Yet, it is strange to note that some churches together with their pastors, though willing enough to adopt the program outlined for the year of evangelism, hesitate to follow through with the stewardship plan as though these were two widely different fields . . . one spiritual and the other secular.

They must go together. One cannot dedicate one's self to the Lord without including his possessions. One cannot make appeals to the unsaved to accept Christ without also encouraging the new believers to consider Christ's appeals in the matter of stewardship. "As ye abound in everything, in faith, in utterance, and knowledge, and in all diligence, and in your love to us, see that ye abound in this grace also" (the grace of giving) (II Cor. 8:7).

IX. *This program of giving brings great blessing.* "But this I say, He which soweth sparingly shall reap also sparingly; and he which soweth bountifully shall reap also bountifully . . . And God is able to make all grace abound toward you; that ye, always having all sufficiency in all things, may abound to every good work" (II Cor. 9:6, 8).[25]

At the beginning one of the more consistent criticisms was the objection to a pledge program. This was anticipated as evidenced by a statement we wrote for the back of an every Sunday bulletin in 1958.

"I am willing to give to the Lord's work but will never make a pledge," is a statment sometimes heard when the appeal for pledges is made.

Why not make a pledge?

God made a pledge and in the fullness of time kept His promise to send His only begotten Son into the world to die as a Savior upon the cross of Calvary. God put that pledge in writing!

Paul accepted pledges and anticipated payment of same.

"Now therefore perform the doing of it; that as there was a readiness to will, so there may be a performance also out of that ye have" (2 Cor. 8:11).

A pledge is an act of faith. It takes no faith to give out of what you already possess. That is an expression of gratitude for past blessings. But to promise something you don't even have yet is an act of confidence in God. You are trusting God for the future and promising to share the blessings you know are still in store.

A pledge is more than a promise—it is a covenant with God. God has already promised to supply all your needs and you covenant with Him, that on the basis of His promise, you will give out what is yet to be supplied.

A pledge is a practical, systematic plan followed in every area of life. A layman wrote the following in a secular newspaper:

"Too bad! The man who never makes a pledge cannot have a telephone in his house, for the telephone company will not put the phone in unless he agrees to pay the bill. The same is true of the electricity, water, and groceries. He cannot be a married man, for he would need to make vows to get married; he cannot own property, for he would have to promise to pay taxes; he cannot be a citizen of the United States, for he would have to pledge to support the government. Yes, you do believe in making pledges, but when it comes to the Lord's work you are just hard up for excuses and this is the only one you can think of on short notice. No pledge, as a rule, means no pay. Be honest with yourself!"

A pledge brings great spiritual blessings in addition to the means with which to keep the promise. The records prove that the most generous givers are not those who give only out of what they have but those who make a covenant with God to give in faith.

"God is able to make all grace abound toward you; that ye, always having all sufficiency in all things, may abound to every good work" (2 Cor. 9:8).[26]

Such an ambitious program, as expected, was not without its critics in the pulpit as well as in the pew. A few pastors (there is always a small minority in the midst), seemed to believe that the freedom and independence of the local church must always be exercised for that freedom to survive. Some were afraid of what the giving might do to the regular income. Others listened to a few members who object every time the question of stewardship is raised. Such were also present a century ago and are ever with us. The tragedy is when pastors and people in congregations where majority should rule are enslaved by a small, vociferous, self-centered minority. One must not overlook the fact, however, that some of the objections were the result of failure to fully understand the plan. Once it was made clear, some of the sincere objectors became the most enthusiastic supporters. This was well attested to by a layman who wrote:

> We did participate, wholeheartedly, all the way. Cautious in the beginning, suspicious of organized and pressure approaches to Scriptural giving, we required additional information and explanations, extra board meetings and special meetings of the general assembly. However, once convinced of the Lord's will and the wholesome approach of the Free Church, we followed the step-by-step procedure recommended.
>
> Better informed by the pre-campaign publicity, we were convinced that the plan was just what we wanted and had, in fact, been trying to design ourselves. It followed closely the ratio of expenditures in our current budget. In addition, it provided funds for much needed expansion in our church and for a greater, more effective outreach at home and abroad. Enthusiasm mounted as the Jubilee Fund Program gave occasion for us to put in words a greater vision for our work which we called OUTREACH and included a Sunday School education building, branch churches, more missionaries, proper support of Free Church activities through the Jubilee Fund and additional full-time workers on the staff.
>
> During the campaign, interest was so great that two inspiring songs were composed, entitled Outreach and Reach Out.
>
> The kick-off banquet and the solicitation were times of joy and refreshment. How we enjoyed having these men of God in our midst. There was not one shadow of embarrassment. Everything was pleasantly dignified and filled with such

spiritual blessing that the experience brought our congregation nearer to the Lord and closer together.[27]

The plan also had the unequivocal support of the more influential leaders. One wrote:

Ever since we had our Jubilee Drive Banquet I have felt like writing a line or two, saying something about what I like about this effort. Let me say at once that it is working out very well here. Our people are responding faithfully and well. For all of this, we are most grateful.

I LIKE the name "Jubilee" rather than "Program for Progress." Of course, I realize that the latter is the larger name or designation, covering the whole program for these significant years. The word "Jubilee" is, after all, a Bible word and has in it something of joy and gladness, as well as a significant celebration. The Year of Jubilee in Israel, was, indeed, a time of rejoicing.

I LIKE the spiritual emphasis that is put upon the Jubilee Program. It is not merely a matter of raising money. There is an emphasis upon spiritual dedication. I can say that all of the Free Church pastors who participated here in the calling put the spiritual emphasis first. This was greatly appreciated by me and all here at the church.

I LIKE that it is a grass-roots movement, many people having a share in it. By this I do not mean to discount large gifts, but rather to emphasize the importance of many people having interest in this and sharing in it by way of giving. This, to me, is a far more healthy situation. Certainly we are amazed at the wonderful results when many people participate.

I LIKE the fact that only Free Church pastors are used in the personal solicitations that follow the banquet. This, I think is both important and well. They know our people best and they have had experience in this in their own churches. I can truthfully say that my fellow pastors who participated here were a blessing to our people.

I LIKE this way of honoring our founding fathers and also paying tribute to the past by preparing and providing for the future. In this way, we are not only looking back and thanking God sincerely for the pioneers, but we are looking ahead and making some provision by the grace of God, for those who will come after us as well. I do believe this is entirely pleasing to the Lord.

I LIKE, finally and most important of all, that in all of this we are earnestly seeking to glorify our Lord and Savior Jesus Christ. If we were seeking some honor for ourselves, we would certainly fail. But, in sincerity and humility, seeking to honor the Lord, we may count on His blessings and His guidance in all of it.

I SINCERELY LIKE our Jubilee Fund Program. I earnestly commend it to our churches. It will prove, I am certain, a spiritual blessing.[28]

Not all comments were that encouraging *before* a campaign began in a local church. Even though approved by the General Conference it became necessary to meet with eighty church boards, either in groups or separately, to sell the local leadership on the plan. One of the unique and often frustrating aspects of the work in the Evangelical Free Church is the absence of any clout in conference decisions as far as affiliated congregations are concerned. An affirmative vote seems to mean—"now it is up to the leadership to persuade our church to go along with the decision." Opposition took strange forms at times. In one city, a few of the leaders left town and stayed away until the local solicitation was over and the pastors participating had left.

Incidentally, the results in that church were far above average. But for every such story there are scores of others—inspiring and sometimes even amusing. Speaking at three hundred banquets and on the same subject each night was strenuous but encouraging. I usually left the next morning while the director, Rev. Ivar Sellevaag, stayed behind to superintend the follow-up. There were so many scheduled that Wilber H. Norton, then president of Trinity, filled a similar role as mine in many places making it possible to hold two banquets at one time. There was one stretch of nearly a month when I had ham and potato salad each night, only to have the same menu broken by a series in turkey country for a week, making us hungry for ham again.

One of the older congregations refused to arrange a banquet. The members thought it worldly to use a dinner to raise money. "Too much like the liberal churches," they said and compromised by arranging an old fashioned Scandinavian Smorgasbord which went far beyond anything experienced at the 299 other banquets. Following that we were moved into the sanctuary to spend the evening talking about money!

One man in another town seemed most negative and gave one of the pastors a hard time. When the pastor was about to leave he was told to wait a moment while the gentleman went into another room and came back with a very large check. "I just wanted to see if you had your information about the Free Church straight," he said.

A widow sat in her living room surrounded by several small children as she said, "I feel so badly because I cannot give." She was told that even 25¢ a week was acceptable to God when it represented her willingness and ability. She literally wept when she realized she could also have a share in a two and one-half million dollar fund drive.

As a soliciting pastor visited in one home, a neighbor lady who attended the church but was not a member dropped in. "I suppose you'll be in to see me next," she said. The pastor remembered that her card had been removed from the file that very morning by the local chairman and pastor with the explanation that she wouldn't be interested. The lady saved the solicitor from a great embarrassment and taught the leaders a lesson when she said, "Give me a commitment card now and I'll save you a visit." She made one of the more substantial pledges in that community.

My own mother called and said, "I see that we are going to have a banquet in our church and if I don't attend or if I don't sign a pledge card someone may come to see me. What kind of business is that? Do you know anything about such a crazy idea?" I told her that we wanted to make sure she had made the decision to say no in her own heart and also to be sure she understood the plan and its purposes. We don't think a pastor or chairman has a right to say, "Don't call on Mrs. Olson. After all, she is a widow on a small pension. Further, she has two sons who are preachers and that dims her prospects of financial help from them should the need arise." That did it. She attended the dinner and made her commitment if for no other reason than to show that giving is as one purposes in his or her own heart and not in the heart or mind of some church leader. The rightness of her motive may be challenged but the procedure was on Biblical grounds.

In addition to the two "mossy myths" already mentioned, the Jubilee Fund Drive exploded two additional illusions. The one was that giving to such a cause could so decrease the income for local, current expenses that the church might be unable to continue. The second was that such an earthly matter as money and spirituality cannot mix.

Only one congregation reported a drop in support for current expenses following the program. Many were the reports from churches which experienced the opposite.

One pastor wrote three months after the program was complete in his congregation, "You would be surprised at what you are capable of doing financially. The pledge system confronts each one with the matter of proportionate giving. This increases individual giving and the weekly contributions into a substantial sum in a year. Even the person with a small annual income can give substantially in this manner and can do it quite painlessly." In response to the fear that non-members, who enjoy the benefits of the church but have reasons for not joining, might be offended, he added, "You would be surprised at the interest the seemingly disinterested people of the constituency really have in the local and national work. Parents of Sunday School children did not object to a systematic method of giving for the improvement of facilities for their children and for the furtherance of the work in which the church is vitally interested. The 'fringe crowd' is more interested in the church's welfare than we sometimes think. We have had some definite examples of this."[29]

Another reported, "Would our people rob Peter to pay Paul? I asked our church financial secretary for the average offering for the three weeks previous to the Jubilee Fund drive. It was $537.94 per Sunday for the general and mission funds. Three weeks after the campaign I received the offering average. It amounted to $618.56! This was a *gain* of $80.62 per Sunday for the general and mission funds, *plus* the offerings which came in each Sunday for the Jubilee Fund. The Jubilee Fund drive has not hurt our finances. It has helped. Last October, just four years after our building project, the church paid off the mortgage on the building, which cost $225,000. The mission budget for 1958 has been increased by an additional $1,000. In all funds, which include the general, mission, Jubilee, Sunday School, Women's Missionary Society and Young People, our total receipts during 1957 were over $95,000."[30]

One pastor wrote of the spiritual blessings and added, "Furthermore, everyone is amazed at the monthly response. Collections for the first six months averaged more than was pledged. Not only this, but our regular weekly offerings for current expenses have exceeded the previous records of the past year."

"Our church was reluctant to go along with the program," wrote another. "We felt that our small group was doing its utmost in giving. Our per captia giving the previous year was about $30 above the Free Church average. Many thought we were giving our limit. After ten months in the program, here are the results: our per capita giving has now gone to $64 above the Free Church average. Our present average monthly income for the Jubilee Fund is running about $38 above the pledges."

Another myth, repeated often in Christian circles, is that drives for money chill the spiritual temperature of a congregation. This was also exploded. The pastors used in the follow-up program were carefully selected. They were experienced in counseling. We discovered early that members who for good reasons may have been reluctant to share personal problems with their own pastor, took advantage of the visitor by seeking his help. There was hardly a local campaign without the brethren reporting praying with individuals either in the matter of salvation or personal spiritual problems. The plan recommended that non-member parents of Sunday School children also be visited. Many of these were not believers, so provided a great opportunity for witnessing. The advance preparation, the appreciation in the hearts of parents for what a local church was doing for the children, the special prayer meetings before the banquet, and the presence of the Holy Spirit opened many hearts to the Gospel. One pastor rejoiced, "Because we gave opportunity to our entire Sunday School constituency to have a share in the program, we are happy to report, in one instance at least, that a nominally interested family has been saved and has recently joined the church. They are just babes in Christ, but hungry and growing—and giving! In addition, there are several other families who, though they have not come through for the Lord, seem to feel 'tied in' with the work since they are given an opportunity to participate in this manner . . . We are also realizing a deepening of the spiritual lives of those who before were purely nominal Christians. This fact is very marked among several families."

Appraisal of the spiritual thrust of the Jubilee Fund drive was summarized by one of the pastors who participated in the solicitation. He expressed what was the conclusion of all members of the team. "Much blessing has come to my soul when attending the fellowship meal which starts each campaign. Many of these gatherings have had not only food for the body but also for the soul. I have noticed that the spiritual note in the banquet is of tremendous help throughout the campaign. One can almost feel the spiritual pulse of the congregation at that time. Let me inject here a bit of advice to churches yet to hold their Jubilee Drives: spend much time in prayer before you even begin the preparation for the campaign. To me, each time of participation is a week of constant prayer for spiritual guidance that I might be a blessing and a help both to the local church and each individual called upon, as well as to our entire world program. The home-to-home visitation is a great challenge and blessing in itself. To hear of people's interest in the Free Church, in Trinity and the work at home and abroad is wonderful. It is also a blessing to sit down in the home and listen to the problems of people; financial, physical and spiritual. More thrilling are the blessings received through answered prayer. At times I leave a home with a burden on my heart for the people. The spirit within me groans with groanings that cannot be uttered for the temporal or spiritual need. It has been a joy to see the response of the people when they understand and know the need. I believe that God is in this Jubilee Program and that it is going to be of tremendous blessing to our churches throughout the world. God is going to glorify Himself and His people are going to know an increase in spiritual joy and blessing."[31]

There were also several other benefits. One church reported an increase of more than thirty percent in the number of members using the weekly envelope system. Several churches were assisted in setting up accounting procedures. One reported, "Another high point achieved through the stewardship program is a greatly improved record system. This has given the church a greater incentive to maintain these records. Needless to say, better records have led to better management of our publicity for the church and Sunday School. As a result of the program it became apparent that we ought to have an addressing machine to follow-up on these contacts. The machine was purchased and has been utilized continuously."

It seemed that we moved from peak to peak. Who could have anticipated that the Jubilee Fund drive would end in a deep valley!

Our final local program was conducted at Ponca, Nebraska, on a Thursday evening (July 14, 1960). Ivar Sellevaag was there to do the soliciting along with the district superintendent. I left after the banquet planning to return for Sunday to help the friends dedicate their new building. Sellevaag was to go to Minneapolis for an appointment on Monday. Finishing his work earlier than anticipated he left Saturday. On Tuesday in Minneapolis I had an unforgettable phone call. "Do you have a minister named Sellevaag in your denomination?" I was asked. When I answered affirmatively, he added, "We have just discovered his body in the Curtis Hotel." It seems that on Sunday he had started to take a shower and was electrocuted. With a "do not disturb sign" on the door, his death was not discovered until two days later. About the same time I received the message that missionary Arthur Lindquist had been killed in a car accident on the same day. It's ironic in one way since Lindquist was the tireless motivator behind the establishment of the Ministerial Pension Fund a few years earlier. Both men died with "their boots on." It can be written of these two servants of Jesus and His Church what John was ordered to write, as recorded in Revelation 14:13: "Blessed are the dead which die in the Lord from henceforth: Yea, said the Spirit, that they may rest from their labours; and their works do follow them." One churchman said years ago, "Blessed are the money raisers for they shall stand next to the martyrs in heaven!"

Sellevaag directed all but two of the campaigns, visiting in more homes of Free Church members than anyone before or after. During the first two years he worked for Chase Associates, the group of evangelical men assisting in the program, and for the final year out of the President's Office. He was uniquely qualified for the task. An immigrant himself, he was the son of one of the founders of the Free Church of Norway and of one of Norway's leading women evangelists.[32] He had broad experience as pastor of three Evangelical Free Churches. During the seventeen years he served as pastor of a Christian Church in New Hampshire he became recognized as a leader among evangelicals in New England. He was one of the founders of the National Association of Evangelicals and was influential in persuading the Norwegian-Danish Free Church to become the first denomination to join following the organizational meeting. He also pioneered in religious broadcasting. His expertise in the Scandinavian languages helped in talking to some of the pioneers still living in the 1950s. He was also a soul winner using the solicitation visits to witness for Christ. One young man converted at that time through the influence of Sellevaag became one of the prime movers in the development of Trinity Western College and also donated the land for one of the churches. The young man was not only born again but reached full maturity in stewardship at the time of his spiritual birth.

But, how soon we are forgotten! In researching on Sellevaag, we could not even find his file in the headquarters morgue and none of the current staff even knew who he was.

We have come a long way from the attitudes toward stewardship reported at the beginning of this chapter. Will the "virtue of generosity" continue to remain among the members in the next generation? It will not be an automatic transfer from one generation to another. The generosity of one generation can no more be passed on than the faith that leads one to salvation. Only the example can be passed on. It behooves leaders to teach the whole counsel of God. Generosity must repeatedly be placed along side faith, utterance, knowledge and enthusiasm. Each new generation must, for itself, recognize that all that they are and all that they have are loaned to them by the Heavenly Father and each must someday give an account of his stewardship.

FOOTNOTES—CHAPTER IV

1. Carlsen, Nils, *Liv og Virksomhet i Herren's Vingaard,* Evangelistens Forlag, Chicago, 1928, p. 106.
2. Ibid., p. 79.
3. Ibid., p. 180.
4. Halleen, E. A., *Sunshine and Shadows, Evangelical Beacon,* Chicago, p. 33, 34.
5. Anderson, A. A., *Twenty Years in the Wild West,* Free Church Publications, Chicago, pp. 33, 34.
6. Ibid., pp. 33, 34.
7. Ibid., pp. 45, 46.
8. *The Golden Jubilee,* 1934, p.36.
9. Halleen, op. cit., pp. 82, 83, 84.
10. Ibid., pp. 100, 101.
11. Phillips, J. B., *The New Testament in Modern English,* The Macmillan Company, New York, 1958.
12. Carlsen, op. cit., p. 227.
13. Ibid., p. 227.
14. Two additional volumes in the Heritage Series by other authors.
15. Yearbook, 1918, p. 52.
16. *Evangelical Beacon,* June 27, 1944.
17. Ibid., August 21, 1945.
18. Carlsen, op. cit., p. 110.
19. Ibid., p. 109.
20. *Evangelisten,* September 3, 1932.
21. Carlsen, op. cit., p. 223.
22. Ibid., p. 224.
23. Loe, Ingvald, J., writing in the *Evangelisten,* September 10, 1932.
24. *Evangelisten,* July 28, 1926.
25. *Evangelical Beacon,* January 14, 1958.
26. Ibid., February 4, 1958.
27. Ibid., May 20, 1958.
28. Ibid., April 5, 1958.
29. Ibid., July 22, 1958.
30. Ibid., February 4, 1958.
31. Ibid., May 20, 1958.
32. The story of Ivar Sellevaag's mother is recorded in the book, *A Woman of Her Times,* by Della E. Olson, under the name Laura Skjellsvik.

Chapter V

MISTAKES GOD USES

Fire, and hail; snow, and vapour; stormy winds fulfilling His word. Psalm 148:8

The stories which appear in this chapter tell of our God not only ruling but overruling in the affairs of men but doing so in many strange ways.

He turns man's mistakes around to His purpose. Apparent defeats can become victories, liabilities can become assets, losses can become gains. The Bible contains many illustrations of a mistake becoming a blessing through divine intervention. For the brothers of Joseph to sell him into slavery was certainly a wrong against the lad and his father, but as Joseph said to those brothers decades later, "As for you, ye thought evil against me; but God meant it unto good, to bring to pass, as it is this day, to save much people alive" (Genesis 50:20). Pharaoh made a mistake in ordering the newly-born Hebrew males cast into the Nile River and thus introducing genocide. The neighbors of the mother of Moses, had they known, would have tried to persuade her not to carry out her plan to defy the mighty Pharaoh. Had she been found out, the entire Hebrew people might have suffered the consequences. But out of that disobedience came the deliverer of the Hebrew nation and the instrument through whom God gave Israel and the rest of mankind the law. Paul planned to carry the Gospel to Bithynia but "the Spirit suffered them not" (Acts 16:7), and as a result the Gospel came to Europe.

A cursory reading of Romans 8:28 in the KJV has lead

many to a faulty conclusion thus missing a great truth. It reads: "And we know that all things work together for good to them that love God, to them that are called according to his purpose." Some have concluded that the experiences of life—successes and failures, joys and sorrows, rights and wrongs can somehow be put in a blender of sorts, mixed together and come out as something different and good but containing the elements of all the experiences. This is true even though some of these are results of our own pride, stubbornness and disobedience while others may have been through no apparent fault of our own. Nor can any experience be blamed on fate.

Some of the other translations provide an exhilarating clarification revealing that it is God who operates the blender. It is He who works through the all things to His glory and gain. "We know that in all things God works for good with those who love him" (TEV). "And we know that God causes all things to work together for good to them that love God" (NAS). "And we know that in all things God works for the good of those who love him" (NIV)."Moreover we know that to those who love God, who are called according to his plan, everything that happens fits into a pattern for good" (JBP).

Yes, it is God who works; God who causes. Things do not work together automatically. God does not cause our mistakes but He does use them for our good. Other Scripture passages also confirm that even in the lives of those who are not aware of God's love for them, God in His love overrules. After all, "We love Him because He first loved us" (I John 4:19).

Not all mistakes can be placed under the category of sins. Some are merely matters of ignorance or poor judgment. Others may be made by a person or group who knows that they are not the best decisions but, nevertheless, the best under the circumstances. For example, churches are sometimes erected on certain lots, not because the location is best, but the land is cheaper or even free. Pastors have been called who may not have been the first choice of the majority but because in their living closer to the location of the church, moving expenses would be less; or he "would come cheaper" as to salary; or some special friends were able to pressure the congregation. Sometimes, second choices are made because a person or congregation lacks the faith or the vision to accept the best.

God's permissive will is not always His perfect will. We will not know until we are fully known how different our own history might have been had we chosen a different path.

But there are occasions when God uses even our mistakes to serve Him.

The history of The Evangelical Free Church of America no doubt contains many such stories. Those told here are limited to events with which I am personally familiar. Even then, just a few are included. It would take an entire volume to record them all. Names are deliberately omitted but not because the churches and people involved would object nor because the accounts are inaccurate. Each has been carefully verified by persons associated with the events who knew the stories would be told. I have felt that a certain amount of anonymity might enhance the stories and permit others to read into them similar experiences.

The word *mistake* in the title may not be appropriate in each case but it does serve as an umbrella.

A FROZEN ASSET

It was 1959. The church was located in a small town in one of the richer farmlands in the midwest. The work was going forward and the membership increasing with the facilities, and as a result becoming more crowded. My own recollection of cramped quarters is when we had to move to a nearby city for the closing day of a conference to meet in its auditorium because there was no longer any room in the church.

An addition to the building was proposed, considered, debated and rejected as being beyond the means of the membership. The estimated cost was $20,000. The budget at that time ran about $7,000 a year. My own experience in over 300 building fund drives has been that in a real need and with an enthusiastic congregation, a majority of the churches easily realized three times their annual budget in a three-year capital funds drive. The group did not wish to try to see what might be available through such a program. Further, the bank refused to loan the money which may have subsequently been needed even though the members were financially substantial and highly reputable farmers in the community.

That was the situation up until Easter week. On Thursday morning one of the members had been into the city a few miles away to meet his daughter who was coming home from Trinity College to spend Easter vacation with her family. Driving by the church at about seven o' clock on a sub zero morning he noticed smoke coming from the building. He hurried to turn on the fire siren to arouse the village and call out the local volunteer fire fighters. But alas! The siren was frozen! The church burned to the ground. Members living out on the farms were not even aware of the loss until they listened to the morning news from a nearby local radio station.

The congregation faced the inevitable. It was no longer a debate over a $20,000 addition since now there was the need of an entire new building. The congregation in faith was up to the challenge. It took only two days for the board to agree on the erection of a new church. Leaders immediately went out to call on the members to solicit cash and pledges. Two of the men, in one day, raised $24,000! The total cost of the new structure was $85,000. It was financed by $33,000 from insurance plus cash and pledges from the members and a loan. No help from the bank was needed as five members, regardless of the lack of faith to launch the $20,000 project, now loaned the remaining required. That loan was shortly paid off.

The Seventy-fifth Anniversary brochure contained this account as written by one of the members:

On a stormy morning on March 26, 1959, our church structure burned. The building and all contents were lost. The only
remaining items are those which were "cast upon the water;"
namely, the platform chairs which had been given to the . . .
Evangelical Free Church and the reed organ which had been
given to the mission field in Venezuela.

The church board met March 28, 1959, and from this meeting
came the recommendation that a new building be con-
structed. The first service after the fire of Thursday was the
Sunday morning Easter service. This was held in the school
auditorium. We all remember that day vividly as it seemed
that a part of each of us had been lost. On April 6th at the
quarterly business meeting of the congregation, the recommendation of the board was accepted and plans were begun to
rebuild. An architect was hired and committees appointed to
make plans for the new building. We continued to hold our
services and Sunday School classes in the school building and
the Sunday evening services were held in the local Methodist
Church.

Ground breaking ceremonies were held July 19, 1959. The
cornerstone was laid December 20, 1959.

Our first service in the new church was held Sunday, March
4, 1960. The dedication was on Sunday afternoon, April 24,
1960.

The suggestion that what was saved was what had been
given away is interesting. The church mentioned was a
home missions project. I am reminded of an experience in
the 1930s. The financial crash and resultant economic
chaos in 1929 brought out many stories. One Free Church
man in Chicago who owned many apartment houses lost
them all and spent the final years of his life working as a
custodian in an apartment house he had built and once
owned. I met him on a downtown stroll and mentioned
having heard of his loss. "But I didn't lose everything," he
responded. "The school and churches I helped erect in
Africa are still serving the Lord."

THE ORGAN PLAYED A DIFFERENT TUNE

To build or not to build, to move to a new location or

stay, to add or to demolish and start over—these questions have troubled and, in some cases, divided congregations. For one congregation the plan to sell, move and build held little promise of succeeding without seriously breaking up the membership into groups, possibly two congregations. One leader, who lived next door to the church and served as custodian, had been a faithful member for years. He did everything possible to hinder a move and discourage others from supporting it. A committee was joined by the district superintendent to visit a prospective site. Upon returning to the church, they found that the brother had prepared strawberry shortcake to serve the committee members to soften them up for his often repeated appeal not to recommend the site. It should be said even before we continue with the narrative that once the events which followed convinced him that the Lord was using the congregation out in the suburb, he continued as one of the congregation's most loyal supporters and remains so at the time of this writing. One said, "We have no member more loyal than he."

The congregation faced the New Year in a state of uncertainty. The members were concerned that the Lord's will might be clear and meet with a united response no matter what it turned out to be—move or stay. The Watchnight service on New Year's Eve of 1967 is recalled as one of the most memorable services in the history of the church. The man who was pastor at that time writes:

> We had candles around a large cross with a candle in the middle to represent Christ, the Light of the World. The first one to come up for a testimony and then to light a candle, broke down as he testified. That was the tenor of the service until well after midnight. Another chap and I were the last to leave the church—all seemed to be well, and all the candles that had been burning around the church seemed to be out.

As the people left the church shortly after midnight they were careful to see that all the candles were extinguished and the lights turned off. The switch for the organ had also been turned off but unbeknown to them an electrical short started a smoldering fire in the beautiful instrument. Neighbors seeing the smoke coming out through the windows turned in the alarm during the wee hours of the morning. It being the night of New Year's Eve, pranksters from the area had turned in a number of false alarms. Consequently, the first alarm was treated as just another prank. By the time the alarm was taken seriously it was too late to save the building. It was completely gutted. Had the first alarm been heeded, only the organ would have been destroyed.

Naturally this was a blow, especially when the insurance coverage was only between $35,000 to $40,000, an amount inadequate for rebuilding.

Further, the plan to sell the building to provide part of the cost for the anticipated new building project was now shattered.

The press reported on the fires with large headlines. The church had never had so much publicity before. "Too bad," said one of the younger members, "that the story could not have been about revival fires instead of a building fire!"

In one sense it could be said that the fire melted the congregation together into a united goal—to move and erect a new building. A special fund raising banquet was planned. The son of the leading promoter of the move to the new location presided. His father, long a pillar in the church, had presided over the congregational meeting when in the midst of the tensions the recommendation to move was rejected. This was done reluctantly for the sake of unity. The leader died shortly after the decision was made and so did not live to see his dream come true. It is interesting to recall that the son of the leader of the opposition became the first chairman of the congregation in the new building and the son of the leader of the group favoring the move became the one to head the financial drive. I participated in the fund appeal at the banquet and predicted a result far beyond his fondest hope. When the results were announced even in excess of my own figure, the young man broke into tears.

The pastor tells of a personal experience in connection with the fire:

An interesting item was that one year before the fire I was run into by a woman who later took me to small claims court. I won the case as she was definitely in the wrong. Through it my insurance company gave me absolutely no help, so I changed companies. In June I met the head man for the new company and he asked "Pastor, do you have insurance on your books and personal effects?" I said I did not, and asked for a policy to cover it. In half a year, I stood in the gutted church, and in a study that looked like a slice out of midnight. But then I had the policy because of the accident on my day-off the previous January. A few days after the fire, the insurance company called saying, "We understand you had several volumes in the fire the other day." "Several volumes!" I said. "Yes, we were told that you had several volumes of theological books in the church fire." Then I said to him, "Well, if over a thousand volumes of theological books is what you consider *several* volumes, that is what I had." When he heard the number of books which were actually in the fire he said, "Holy Smoke!" When I thought about what kind of books were involved, I thought his answer was quite appropriate.

ALL OR NOTHING

One of our oldest congregations received its first building in a most unusual way. This happened long before 1884. There was a Lutheran Church in the town patterned after the State Church of Sweden. The pastor was invited to attend some Gospel meetings in a nearby town where he was converted as were several of the members. This divided the congregation so that the new believers decided to form a separate congregation. Being honorable people they made a proposition to the rest, "Since we represent about half of the congregation, we make two propositions. The one is that you give us fifty percent of the appraised value of the building and we will leave and build a new church. The second is that we pay you half of the value and take over the building." The others were opposed to both ideas and sued the group of new believers for sole ownership of the building. This was before the church constitutions were so written as to protect the party remaining true to the local constitution, etc.

The believers repeated before the judge their "fifty-fifty" offer. Then the judge asked the other members, "What's your offer or counter proposal?" They replied, "All or nothing." The judge ruled, "You then get nothing." That is how one of the original Swedish Evangelical Free Churches got its first meeting place.

NOT ALWAYS AN ILL WIND

In their haste to move out of school houses, rented halls and church buildings, some congregations didn't think far enough ahead to the future location of streets and parking lots or the need for kitchen and toilet facilities, etc. One such congregation erected a small building without excavating for a basement. In due time, a basement was needed and the structure was placed on stilts in preparation for digging new footings and foundation. A controversy arose because some felt that the building should be moved a few feet farther down the road but the final decision was to leave it where it was. That night a strong wind arose and blew across the open, flat countryside. The building toppled to the ground as the stilts could not stand against the pressure. In the morning the structure was found to be unharmed but a few feet back from where it had originally stood.

GREAT WAS THE FALL OF IT

The *Evangelical Beacon* called the story a moving experience but it was much more than that.

A newly formed congregation had a choice between erecting a new church home or accepting an older building which was available at little or no cost providing it would continue to serve as a church. The only problem was that it had to be moved twelve miles, but to the enthusiastic group this presented a challenge rather than a problem.

151

On September 16, 1965, the flock met on a rainy evening to break ground on a new site consisting of four acres. By November the foundation was completed as were also negotiations with the utility companies and the railroad for the temporary cutting of electric and telephone wires to facilitate the move across the tracks.

All things were now ready. November 4th was the date chosen for the big move. But alas, as the mover was raising the church on to his trucks, the building fell apart! It was a total loss. Apparently the old wooden building, through the decades, had been erected piecemeal and in several stages.

Now the congregation faced a new challenge, one which was rejected before. As the *Beacon* put it, "This new and struggling group now finds it necessary to build entirely new on the foundation." The article closed with an appeal for prayer on behalf of the congregation.

People across the country responded with more than prayer. The undertaking became Shareholders Project number 49. The Shareholders program along with the Christian Investors Foundation are, in themselves, signs of reaching maturity.

By September 11, 1966, the first phase of the building was completed. It measured 34' x 50' with an auditorium seating 180, six classrooms, pastor's study, mothers' room, Sunday School office and kitchen. In June of 1980 there was a second dedication service when the final phase of the building program was completed.

THE CASE OF THE MISSING BATTERIES

This story is not unique but the circumstances and unusual events surrounding it are different from any other.

It happened to one of the oldest and historic congregations. The church, organized in 1897, erected its first building in 1903 and by 1923, facing conditions similar to what it would again face nearly fifty years later, sold the building and erected a new structure in an attractive area not far from the center of the city. This city is also the location of one of America's oldest and most prestigious universities. The congregation was progressive and in tune with the changing times and passed through the change in language from Scandinavian to English before it was too late. The next generation followed in the footsteps of their fathers. Recognizing the changing population pattern in the community, it sought to minister to the minorities, especially the blacks, which resulted in a number of children from the neighborhood attending. Members, however, gradually moved from the immediate neighborhood.

After forty-seven years the congregation had to face the question of whether or not to follow the members to a location elsewhere. There were the usual arguments against a move. First, there were those who wished to stay for sentimental reasons. Many had been converted there. They could look at certain pews and recall with gratitude their parents' past role in that building. They could point to rooms in the church and adjacent houses which were acquired throughout the years where they had heard the Word in the Sunday School classes. Others were opposed on the grounds that in moving they would be running away from a responsibility to witness to the new people in the community. This was hardly a legitimate argument since their history shows that they had not only accepted that challenge but had been comparatively successful. The third source of opposition came from those who were enamored with the proximity of the university. True, some members of the faculty and a few students attended and some of these were active in the work of the church, but their stay was transitory.

The members became concerned lest the unity be broken when a series of related events crystallized the various opinions into the feeling that a move was imperative.

First there were break-ins and other forms of vandalism.

Files were rifled, papers scattered and equipment damaged. One day as the pastor was meeting with the confirmation class, a stone was thrown through the window of the study. Cars were damaged. Two couples were mugged. One of the men was not only a leader in the church but also in denominational affairs. As the mugger grabbed the wife's handbag he also reached for what he thought was her billfold. It turned out to be a New Testament! It became no longer safe to attend services after dark. In fact, there were even risks involved in daylight. Then came the last straw! As the members of the congregation and visitors who had driven from other towns came out of the church after attending a concert they found that the batteries had been stolen out of several cars. That did it!

The hand of God was evident in many ways once the congregation came to a prayerful, united and firm decision to move. A search committee had already inspected twelve possible sites in the event the decision of the church would be in favor of moving. None of these seemed to bring to the search committee the feeling that "this is the place." On the very afternoon of the church meeting a property was found that seemed to be just what was needed and at a price within the means of the congregation. In addition to voting in favor of a move, the meeting authorized the purchase of site number thirteen although it was not located in the suburb to which most of the members had moved. A study of the churches in the community which revealed there were already evangelical churches there, but none in the town of the accepted location, became an important factor in choosing site number thirteen. However, the next day they discovered that a developer had taken a thirty-day option on the property. The discovery that the desirable land was not available did not cause panic. The congregation had been in the old building nearly half a century and they could stay longer while waiting on the Lord for further guidance. At the end of the thirty days, the prospective buyers surrendered the option. The church then bought the building at a price over ten percent less than the price demanded a month earlier and with the interest on the required loan also reduced. Funds for payment of the entire cost would not be available until the old building was sold.

Whatever concerns may have existed as to the question, "Who would buy the building?" were soon dissipated. There were six groups seeking to purchase the property once the decision to move became known. The congregation approved with deep satisfaction the · sale to an evangelical black congregation which would continue to preach the Gospel in that place and in a more capable manner in spite of the sincerity and efforts of the departing group. There was another interesting development. The new church was not much more than a blueprint by the time the building was sold. Arrangements were made with the new owners to share the building. This accommodation lasted for eighteen months and led not only to an occasional combined meeting but a better understanding on the part of both congregations of the problem each faced. They had much in common. As one leader told me, "The arrangement worked beautifully." Today there is an effective Christian ministry in two places rather than one. Certainly God did not inspire the vandalism, the tragic, painful muggings, nor the wholesale stealing of batteries but, as in so many instances, He did lead the people to a decision and revealed His hand as the members moved step-by-step until the move was completed. He also was with them and has worked through them in the new location.

THE BANKER'S MISTAKE

There was a time when banks could blame mistakes on employees, as I well remember for I once worked in a banking institution. Times have changed. Now mistakes are blamed on computers and it often takes several employees to correct them. This story is B.C.—before computers. I was quite disturbed on my first visit to this congregation. The building was an unfinished 20 X 36 foot structure covered with tar paper, with the quarters for the pastor in what was more of a cellar than a basement—cold and damp. I still remember his child walking around coughing and with a running nose. There was little chance of recovering under such conditions.

The congregation had reached 119 in attendance, necessitating consideration being given to enlarging the unfinished structure or starting a new building. There was a lot across the street available for $1500. The building fund contained $900 but the bank would not loan the church the additional money required. The church was not yet organized. Finally, the bank yielded on the condition that the group provide five co-signers for a note. "This," as the pastor at that time (1960) writes, "hurt our pride so we waited with our proceedings."

The pastor continues:

> On a Friday evening my treasurer came to me with a letter from the bank informing him that $10,000 had been deposited to the church account. We agreed to say nothing about it over the weekend but to wait and check things on Monday. On our visit to the bank, we were informed that the money had come by Western Union from Minneapolis (the location of The Evangelical Free Church headquarters). We were not expecting any money as we had not requested any but who were we to argue with the Lord's provision! We bought the lot with part of the money, and only the beginning of winter stopped us from beginning to build.

In the meantime the Lutherans were erecting a new church building across the street. Unbeknown to the Free Church people, though the Lutherans continued to proceed with the building, they were desperately in need of the cash promised them by the Evangelical Lutheran Church with headquarters also located in Minneapolis. They wrote and telephoned. Finally the Evangelical Free Church received a second letter from the bank stating that a terrible mistake had been made. The money was intended for the Lutherans and not the Evangelical Free Church! The rationalization was that since Evangelical Free comes before Evangelical Lutheran in the alphabetical listing of churches, the error was plausible.

The events which followed are also interesting. The District Superintendent called upon the head of the bank in another town who had jurisdiction over the bank where the mistake was made and asked him what he should tell the bank officials where the error had occurred. He replied, "Thank them and ask them what the bank (not the congregation) proposes to do about the problem!" The response included a series of moves initiated by the bank. Since the bank had refused a loan in the first place they entered it as an overdraft in the Evangelical Free Church account. However, the bank could not penalize the church for the overdraft since it was its mistake. Second, the congregation discovered that under pressure they had faith to do the impossible and raised funds to proceed with the building program. The bank, either from embarrassment or in seeing a new potential in the young congregation, responded to the need for meeting the overdraft, by granting a building loan of $12,000. The group was also able to borrow an additional $5,000 while raising $10,000 in cash, providing the $27,000 to construct the new church. The contractor, a member of the Lutheran Church across the street, erected both buildings.

It was my privilege to return to that city for a Jubilee Banquet later when funds were committed to reduce the mortgage. There was also an element of the miraculous in that visit. There was a low and heavy cloud covering the whole area. The pilot of the plane on which I was arriving was about to give up trying to land after circling for an hour when suddenly and momentarily a hole appeared in the clouds enabling him to see the ground and the city which was surrounded by mountains.

A RIGHT TURN ON THE WRONG STREET

So far we have shared accounts of buildings, fires, winds and freezing temperatures. God also overrules in the personal lives of individuals. Elijah revealed to the people of his time that God of heaven could answer by fire. Later, while hiding in a cave for fear of Jezebel, he discovered that God was not only working through a fire:

> And he said, "Go forth, and stand upon the mount before the Lord." And, behold, the Lord passed by, and a great and strong wind rent the mountains, and brake in pieces the rocks before the Lord; but the Lord was not in the wind: and after the wind an earthquake; but the Lord was not in the earthquake;

> And after the earthquake a fire; but the Lord was not in the fire: and after the fire a still small voice (I Kings 19:11, 12).

The city in which the church of this story is located is the site for one of our nation's Air force bases. Young men and women come there from all parts of the United States.

One young man made inquiries as to the address of a church belonging to the same denomination as his church back home. He was told to walk so many blocks, then turn right and he'd find the chuch within a couple of blocks. Somehow (or was it providentially) he lost count of how many blocks he had walked and turned right too soon and there it was just as the informant had told him. But it was not the same as the church of his childhood. It was an Evangelical Free Church. It was quite different. He did not fully understand the chief difference immediately—the Gospel of salvation through faith in Jesus Christ was preached. The people were different, too, in that they were so friendly to a lonely service man. The Holy Spirit, through the preaching of the Word of God, the Christian hospitality of the members of the congregation, and exemplary lives of the young people eventually convinced him they all had something he did not have. The result was that he became a believer.

Several years later, at a special celebration, he returned to give his testimony and for the first time his new friends from military days heard the story of the right turn on the wrong street. God uses man's mistakes.

THE RIGHT RITE—THE WRONG CHURCH

The founders of The Evangelical Free Church of America and the pioneers, in establishing congregations, did not abandon all of the practices of the Lutheran State Churches when they left them. In this they followed the Scriptural admonition, "Prove all things; hold fast to that which is good" (I Thess. 5:21). The test for all doctrine and deportment was the Scriptures. "Where stands it written?" (Huru Staar Det Skrevet?) was the battle cry in all controversies. The great teachings of the Reformation— justification by faith, every man a priest, the Scriptures and not the church as the final authority, the divine inspiration of the Bible—stood written in God's Holy Word.

The same held true regarding certain practices of the church. Though the rite of marriage had to conform to the laws of the State, the ceremony was sacred and belonged to the Church. Presenting children to God as infants followed a long history of a practice going back to the beginning of Christianity in Scandinavia, with or without baptism. The Lord's Supper was not to be dropped just because the Church had abused it.

The was also true regarding the rite called confirmation. Some have been afraid to use the word because both Catholic and Protestant churches included, as they did to baptism and the Lord's Supper, meanings not acceptable to the new believers. They refused to accept the teaching that in these rites the participant could obtain salvation or that the priest or pastor had authority to grant or deny the same.

Many names have been used as a substitute for confirmation while seeking to keep "that which is good." Some pastors have dropped the practice altogether, a tragic mistake as manifested in the Bible illiteracy among many who profess faith in Christ.

The confirmation class, conducted by the pastor or associate, is for young people as they reach their early teens. The course marks a shift from Bible stories to doctrine including the theological position of the local congregation and denomination. It brings the young people into closer acquaintanceship with the pastor during the most crucial time of their lives—adolescence. It is one of the more successful methods of winning youth to Christ with the pastor meeting weekly with them for a period of one or two years. With the pastor, parents, and church making much over the course at the time of graduation, the young people, too, begin to realize its importance. As one gets older and he reminisces about his earlier days in the Church, the period when he "studied for the pastor," or as the grandparents put it, "read for the preacher" (lese for presten) seems to remain most vivid in his memory. Some memories are humorous, some are sad, some are blessed.

We leave the story of the confirmation in the "wrong church" temporarily to share the beautiful account of E. A. Halleen's confirmation as told in his autobiography.

Childhood's days are before my eyes. I am watching a little solemn-faced boy sitting crouched in a corner listening to the divine service. The minister is standing in front of the altar, and is intoning the exhortations devoutly. The choir in the gallery is chanting the responses. The organ thunders out and floods through the building majestically. I am rapt in an ecstasy of sweet terror, for the Lord God is coming down upon us. He is standing before me and touching my body, so that I have to close my eyes in a terror of shuddering ecstasy.

—Author Unknown.

It was Easter Sunday in 1889. The sun rose undimmed. The lilacs were blooming; birds were singing. It was confirmation day. Long before the church bells sent their melodious tones over the fragrant vales, calling the folks to worship, we were gathered in the church vestry. The shepherd was giving the final exhortations. Thirty-two boys and girls were listening more or less attentively. There was a tense excitement in the room. Then the bells pealed forth again and we marched in. The congregation was standing; the organ caressed our souls with sweet music. We were soon standing in our appointed places. Then we were seated. As the pastor knelt before the altar, a great hush gripped the audience.

To me this hush was appealing, fostering a spirit of reverence. It was like the hush before the throne of heaven. The rehearsal was on. Questions were put to us in an unusually tender voice. At least I thought they were. But as I was the pastor's pet pupil it may have been the sense of loss of fellowship that caused the feeling.

* * * * * *

The Holy Spirit took occasion again to speak to me very definitely. How quietly He spoke to my soul! Tenderly He brought to my inner vision the glory of being a Christian. It seemed so desirable to make the supreme decision then and there. So possible to make the surrender. And it would have been made had the opportunity been given. However, the seed had been sown. Spiritual values remain. The eternal verities remained even during the years of stubborn rejection that followed. Thank God for that![1]

Some people date their conversions from confirmation time. Those were the years of decision. Such is the story that follows.

It begins with a pastor who proved all things; held fast to that which was good. Traditions that hold value should not be abandoned but used to further the cause. People who excuse themselves by saying, "we don't believe in tradition because we follow the Bible," overlook the fact that not all of them are bad. In fact, the Scriptures distinguish between the tradition of men (see Col. 2:8) and those taught by the apostles. "Therefore, brethren, stand fast, and hold the traditions which ye have been taught, whether by word, or our epistle" (II Thess. 2:15). The pastor referred to announced through the secular press, not just the church bulletin, when the new confirmation class would begin. He also made a clear distinction between separation and isolation. He was involved in the life of the community. His name was well-known to its citizens.

As the son of a couple with a Lutheran background but no church connection reached confirmation age, the mother was anxious that he attend a confirmation class. She selected the Evangelical Free Church. Although she had never attended the church herself, a relative was a member. It was a large church, how could it be anything but Lutheran? It did conduct confirmation classes. The pastor was well-known in the community and to her a "good man." So the son was enrolled in the class but it was not Lutheran.

The confirmand writes, "The pastor taught me all the Scriptures needed for salvation and my mother made sure I memorized them all."

In response to a question as to if and why he continued to attend the church though prior to confirmation he had no connection with any church, he responded, "I did continue attending Sunday School and church because of the influence of the pastor and the youth group there." The relationship between a busy pastor of a large church and a lad who had never attended church developed during those hours in class. The pastor thought the class was important enough not to leave it to an assistant, youth leader, or deacon. How right he was in chosing his priorities!

Following high school the young man attended the University of Illinois. During that time God permitted him to come into a personal crisis with no place to go for help but to God, and remembering what the "pastor taught me in the confirmation class, I accepted Christ."

He later enrolled at Bob Jones University and obtained a degree in Business Administration. Sensing a call from the Lord to enter the Christian ministry, he completed work for a degree in theology. Later, after serving Free Church congregations in the United States and Canada, he took an additional year of studies at Trinity Evangelical Divinity School.

A BROKEN NECK AND A CONTRITE SPIRIT

In a letter granting permission to share his story in this book, the friend wrote; "I have no reservation about your using me as an example in your new book. It reminds me of some graffiti I noticed in one of the factories when I worked for Westinghouse to the effect, 'Don't be discouraged if you're a failure in life, because you can always serve as a bad example.' Seriously, it is exciting on occasion to look back and remember with some embarrassment all of the dumb things we have done over the years and to remember God's grace and blessings in spite of these early excesses."

He attended Sunday School in an Evangelical Free Church and as a child made what he referred to as his initial commitment to Christ and later went forward at a youth meeting at the age of sixteen. However, there was an apparent lack of submission to the Lordship of Jesus Christ. He joined the Navy following completion of high school and in 1946, following his release from the service, enrolled in Steven's Institute of Technology to study Mechanical Engineering. It was during summer vacation the following year (1947) as a brash young man of twenty-one that he attended the annual summer youth conference of the Evangelical Free Church. He arrived with the proverbial chip on his shoulder. His ego was bruised by the fact that he was turned down for a date by a young lady who had attracted his attention. There was more to it than that. There was a revival in the camp. Many young people were committing their lives to Christ which also contributed to his anger. He got into a fight with some of the young men and hit one over the head with a flashlight. He left the camp in a fit of rage but not before his own pastor had taken note of his determination to leave and warned him that he wouldn't be able to run away from God and would probably later regret leaving the conference.

Trying to run away from God was his first mistake. The second was to drive while angry and the third was to drive recklessly. Not far from the conference grounds he was involved in an accident in which his neck was broken. He was eventually taken to a hospital in his own community. "I remember," he recalled, "being so embarrassed and upset that I instructed the nurses not to admit anyone, especially Christians from the Evangelical Free Church. I was still mad and embarrassed about the whole incident."

However, the members of the church, his Sunday School teacher in particular, were faithful in praying for him and witnessing to him and as he put it, "just caring for me." On another occasion he noted, "Obviously, there was a continued strong influence on my life from men in the church, such as my Sunday School teacher who showed an interest in me and provided a role model as well as encouragement." This teacher, together with some other Free Church men, were interested enough in him to offer part-time employment upon his release from the Navy in 1946 while he attended the Institute of Technology. During that period he became acquainted with other Free Church young people. One of these invited him to join him as a student at Taylor University, a Christian school.

It was at that school that he made the final and most significant commitment "in which I responded so strongly to the teaching and influence of the faculty and students . . . I met my wife there. In retrospect I can see the truth of the Scriptural promise in Isaiah 61:3, 'He will give us beauty for ashes.' "

He continued in his studies and earned a doctorate in Education from Indiana University in 1965 after a master's degree from Boston University in 1959. He held many positions at a number of universities. From 1967-1969 he served as Vice President for Administration at Trinity College. From there he went to Wheaton College where, at this writing (1981), he is Vice President for Student Affairs.

His recognition of God's grace and appreciation of the influence by the members of the church in his youth has not dimmed during the years: "I know there were lots of people who were a blessing to me from the church. As I look back over the years, I really am thankful to the Lord for the blessing that the Evangelical Free Church has been to me in my life. I think it strange too, to realize that the same confused, mixed-up, young kid would eventually be Chairman of the Elders at the _____ Evangelical Free Church" (one of the largest congregations in the denomination. ATO).

Yes, God uses man's mistakes. "In all things God works for good with those who love Him." But, as we have noticed in these vignettes God works through people—parents, pastors, Sunday School teachers and other believers.

TWO WRONGS MADE A RIGHT

The older congregations were not always organized under the name Evangelical Free Church. Rather, they came up with many, sometimes strange, titles. They even changed their names several times as they struggled to find one which would truly express the character, structure and purpose of their congregation. The Swedish churches had the same problem in choosing names. The Norwegian-Danish congregations usually started out as Norwegian-Danish Congregational Church, reflecting the aid in personnel and finances provided by the American Congregational Home Mission Society in the early days.

Not all the Norwegian-Danish churches took the name congregational. One exception was a group started, as were many, by a Norwegian immigrant layman. The first name used was The Norwegian Christian Missionary Society (1886) and changed to Christian Free Assembly nearly four months later. It is also interesting to note that the first church building was named *Prayer House* (1889) after the "Bede Hus" name used in Norway.

Eventually, the believers took the name, Evangelical Church, omitting the word Free. We have often, in friendly discussions, talked of how the name as it stands could lead to the assumption that the church might belong to some other denomination. On the other hand, there are now several congregations going by names other than the Evangelical Free Church, right or wrong. Our claim, at least for the sake of this story, is that it was wrong though, of course, permissible under the congregational system.

A young man who anticipated graduation from the university took a job with the J.C. Penney Company in a certain city. Just before graduation his assignment was providentially changed to another city. Shortly after he reported for work his boss, a Presbyterian, noting the man was alone in a strange city, thought it would be a good thing if he attended church. When asked his church affiliation, he gave the name of his childhood church which he hadn't attended since high school days—The Evangelical and Reformed. The boss was sure there was one in the city and letting his fingers walk through the section on churches in the telephone directory, he came across the—Evangelical Church. There it was. But that was the second mistake. It was not an Evangelical and Reformed Church. On this employee's behalf he telephoned the pastor who came to the store on a Saturday afternoon to invite the young man to church. The pastor knew his was the wrong church but also knew that the man would receive little Bible teaching in the other church. He even arranged to personally pick him up early the next morning and continued to do so for several weeks.

The first Sunday morning, to the visitor's surprise, a young lady he had met in the office of the store a few days earlier as she was seeking employment, was the soloist. He found not only a pastor, busy though he was, taking time to show interest in a lonely young man, but a congregation equally hospitable. He was so impressed that he returned for the evening service even though, as he remarked to the pastor at the coffee hour following the evening service, he had missed the repeating of the Apostles' Creed and the

Lord's Prayer at the morning worship. There was another reason for continuing to attend the church and that was the young lady who sang the solo that first Sunday morning. He had his first date with her the next Friday evening. What happened then can best be told by the man himself:

It proved to be league night at the bowling alley so we sat and watched instead of bowling. We began to get acquainted and one of her first questions was, "Are you a Christian?" I responded, "What do you think I am, a heathen?" I meant that I was dressed in a shirt and necktie and was an American. I wasn't roaming through the jungle with spear in hand and a loin cloth. Of course I was a Christian. It was then that Shirley began to tell me what a Christian is and about the personal relationship God wants with each person. I had been baptized as a baby, had gone through catechism as a young teen and joined the church, but faith had never been either personal or real to me. I was intrigued at what she said.

The following weeks we saw our relationship develop and friendships with her family and the church fellowship grow. From September 1949 to January 1950 I was under the hearing of the fine expository preaching of the pastor and the caring fellowship of the Free Church. On January 8, 1950, I made my decision for Christ as the pastor showed me John 1:12: "Yet to all who received him, to those who believed in his name, he gave the right to become children of God" (NIV).

That year was a year of spiritual growth. Shirley and I were married on September 2, 1950. In November of that year, as I was getting settled in my new job as manager of the first floor of the store, our missionary conference caused me to feel God beginning to call me to Christian work. In January my mind was settled and I resigned and went to Chicago to enter Trinity Seminary.

The day I enrolled I called my wife only to hear I had received a present that day—order for active duty. I was a reserve 2nd Lieutenant of Artillery and the Korean War was under way. Instead of Seminary I spent nearly two years in training and serving as a Forward Observer and later Battery Executive Officer for A Battery, 39th Field Artillery Battalion, Third Infantry Division in North Korea. While in Korea I enrolled in Fuller Theological Seminary in Pasadena, California, where we settled after my discharge.

Upon graduation he became pastor of an Evangelical Free Church congregation and since then has served two additional congregations as well as on a district board and as director of one of the largest summer conference programs in the country.

MISTAKES IN THE MILITARY

It was my privilege to serve in the Army of the United States during part of World War II. The experiences of that period would fill another volume. Reported here are three incidents revealing other ways in which God overrules and converts the mistakes of men into channels of blessing.

A JEWISH CHAPLAIN

On completing chaplain's training on the campus of Harvard University I was ordered to Camp Robinson, Arkansas, and the 66th Black Panther Infantry Division. Contrary to the record of many, I stayed with the same unit throughout the two years and even now, over thirty-five years later, am the Chaplain for the Panther Veteran's Organization.

When I reported to the Chief Chaplain of the Division and said, "Chaplain Olson reporting for duty as ordered, sir," he looked at the crosses on the lapels of my uniform and replied, "With the name Olson and the crosses on your uniform, how can you be the Jewish Chaplain?" He then showed me the telegram from Washington promising the Division a Chaplain to serve the many Jewish men in the unit. "What am I going to say to the men now after telling them a Chaplain was on the way and he turns out to be an Olson. Maybe you should meet with them and try to mollify their complaints. Let's announce a Jewish service for Saturday morning and you try to work things out."

In the Army, a suggestion becomes an order. I found a young officer of Jewish background and suggested he help me by reading the Scripture for the day and the appropriate prayer. This also became an order. After the reading, I introduced myself as one of the military's many mistakes and offered to share with them a story of one of the Jewish heroes in their Bible and draw some lessons from his life.

The first response was cool but not icy, especially after I informed them I was from New York from which the majority of them had also come. From then I was known to them as Chaplain Olsonstein—not Chaplain Ole as I was to the rest.

God turned the mistake to an advantage. I held many services for them, became the confidant of several, and when I was asked to give the memorial address for seven (one of whom was a Jew) lost in a training exercise, that provided an additional opportunity to meet Jewish families of the soldiers.

Several of them became so friendly that they attended Protestant services in the front lines during combat just to meet the Chaplain and listen to the ten minute devotionals. Through the Army's mistake there developed during the war an understanding and appreciation of the Jewish community which has grown through the years until it has reached a friendship with the top leaders of the State of Israel.

THE CHAPLAIN A PRISONER OF WAR

Early in my association with the Division, I joined the regiment to which I was assigned for training maneuvers. I was then still an unknown and wondered how I could ever be anything else. Since I was not assigned my own jeep and driver until we went into combat, I was ordered to ride with the officer in charge of the Signal Unit. Incidentally, he was also a Jew and from New York and we developed a good friendship.

As the regiment moved forward in a simulated attack on another regiment, the Signal Corps officer was to stay back by the phone until a call came through that the mission had been accomplished and new lines of communication established. Upon receiving such word, he was to disconnect the phone, pick up some of the wire and proceed by jeep to the new command post with the Chaplain as a rider. With the driver this made three.

During the time of no communication, and unbeknown to us, our regiment had been forced several hundred yards back and we found ourselves forward of our unit and "captured" by some soldiers from the other side. They were quite excited over their catch and took us to the command post of the "enemy." It was getting dark. The chow truck arrived and one officer after the other picked up his mess gear and proceeded out of the tent to get his supper. We three had not eaten since morning so even the idea of an army meal in the field appealed to us but no one offered us anything. They just sat there eating as they interrogated us.

It was past midnight and a cold night it was, when they brought us to an abandoned farm house which had windows with no glass. We felt around on the floor in the dark for a clear place to lie down and found broken glass everywhere so thought it best to try sleeping sitting against a wall. Two guards were posted outside. In the early hours of the morning a truck pulled up. The driver said to the guard, "What a night! I've been all over camp trying to scare up blankets for your prisoners and could get only about forty. How many prisoners have you got in there anyway?" When the guard replied that there were only three, the night was filled with cursing, the likes of which I have not heard before or since.

By morning the maneuvers were ended and the enemy division ordered back to camp and likewise our own but with three men missing in action. We were abandoned by our guards and compelled to walk three miles back to camp since our jeep had been temporarily confiscated.

How did these events work together for good? The camp newspaper picked up the story of the captured Chaplain and drew a cartoon on the cover depicting a Chaplain of the other unit, tall and thin enough to be known as Skinny, sitting with his mess gear piled high with food while the former "prisoner of war" was sitting tied to a tree as steaks with wings were flying all around him but beyond his grasp. The result was instant fame. Now the men knew who that new officer was and that he had not been sitting behind the desk in the camp chapel but had been with them during the field training exercise.

Some would grin as they saluted when passing and others even had courage enough to say, "Hi, Chappy." The attendance at chapel the next Sunday increased greatly and continued at a high level throughout the months which followed. More men came for counseling. In the meantime, the Colonel in command of the other regiment came in person together with his aid to apologize to me, in the presence of others, saying it was all a mistake. "They should never have taken and held a Chaplain." This apology was published in the paper. I was also his guest for a sumptuous dinner at the officers' club. Word about this soon spread around the regiment to the delight of the soldiers. Again, God used a mistake.

THE CHAPLAIN IS DEAD!

It happened on Christmas Eve. The Battle of the Bulge was raging on the European continent. Just before lunch at a camp in England, the Commander's staff met to be briefed on plans to leave for the continent in a week and to discuss plans for the Christmas observation. After lunch we were called back and informed that the entire division, about 15,000 men, were to leave by 6:30 p.m. that same night. As the troopship, the Leopoldville, a ship know to pioneer Free Church missionaries, neared the French harbor of Cherbourg after crossing the English Channel from Weymouth at about six minutes before Christmas Eve 1944, it was hit by either an enemy mine or torpedo. I talked to one survivor recently who insists he saw the wake of a torpedo just before the explosion. The tragedy at sea resulted in the loss of 802 of the 2,237 soldiers aboard, many of whom had become personal friends and not a few fine Christians.[2]

The remainder of the division, some from the troopship and the others off from landing craft, was ordered to Rennes where a temporary camp was set up to regroup and receive new supplies of weapons. It was at that time that my Commander asked me to go back to Cherbourg and call upon those who had been taken to the hospital because of exposure in the chilly waters. I was to bring them his greetings and "say anything that in your opinion is appropriate."

I did not know that the rumor at the hospital was that Chaplain Olson along with another Protestant Chaplain had gone down with the Leopoldville.

This hearsay explains why the man in the first bed of the first ward, upon seeing me, turned pale, leaped from the bed, ran into the next ward saying loudly, "Who said Chaplain Ole was dead?" It was as emotional a reunion as one can expect amongst soldiers entering combat. God even used the rumor. Even a false report that a Chaplain had been lost seemed to inspire greater appreciation of the living presence of one who reminded them of home, family and church. Attendance at services in the front lines during the months we were in actual combat was severely restricted to six or ten persons at a time for reasons of personal safety and collective security but men started attending whom I had not seen before.

All this has contributed to an ongoing relationship. At the reunions of the veterans every two years, the members and their wives insist on a chapel service before they separate at noon on Sunday. It is attended by Protestants, Catholics, Jews and some who may have no church affiliation. A few may even have been drinking heavily the night before but get up for the service, nevertheless.

When the Arnold T. Olson Chapel on the campus of

Trinity Evangelical Divinity School was under construction many of the 1800 members of the P.V.O. contributed funds. Several of the veterans with their wives, led by the president of the organization, attended the dedication of the Chapel on February 9, 1979. In his remarks the president mentioned that they were survivors of the disaster on the English Channel, the first time it had been mentioned publicly in over thirty years. The men, while sharing many stories from their World War II experiences, had always stopped short of referring to the sinking of the Leopoldville. One of the most savoring and memorable experiences in a life filled with many high points became mine when, on behalf of the veterans, I was presented with a plaque stating, "On this your very special day, the dedication of the Arnold T. Olson Chapel, we your buddies at the 66th Infantry Division extend our heartiest congratulations, best wishes and God's blessings."

It is doubtful that without the three mistakes and the way in which God used them such an abiding relationship could have been established.

FOOTNOTES—CHAPTER V

1. Halleen, E. A., *Sunshine and Shadow,* Evangelical Beacon, Chicago, 1944, p. 59, 60.
2. Sanders, Jacquin, *A Night Before Christmas,* G. P. Putnam's Sons, New York, 1963, is the story of the sinking of the Leopoldville.

Chapter VI

HEROES NEVER KNOW IT

" . . . with all my fellow laborers, whose names are in the book of life." (Phil. 4:3b)

The Apostle Paul often included personal greetings in his Epistles. Some of his co-workers, however, remain forever anonymous as far as earthly records are concerned. The same is true today. We have written much about some of the twentieth century heroes of the faith. But there are others whose names didn't even appear in local church bulletins except when their deaths were reported. It was written of Apollos that "he helped them much which had believed through grace" (Acts 18:27). We name schools, churches, cities and streets after Paul. We name our sons and daughters (Pauline) after Paul but I have yet to meet a man named Apollos! He left no epistles, organized no churches, founded no colleges, wrote no books. There is no report of attendance records having been broken in evangelistic crusades. All he did was help those who had come to the faith. Yet Paul aligned himself with him when he wrote, "Who then is Paul, and who is Apollos, but ministers by whom ye believed, even as the Lord gave to every man. I have planted, Apollos watered; but God gave the increase. So then neither is he that planteth anything, neither he that watereth; but God that giveth the increase. Now he that planteth and he that watereth are one: and every man shall receive his own reward according to his own labour" (I Cor. 3:5-8).

Apollos was a saint with a sprinkling can. He made it easier for the young plants to grow. There's nothing spectacular about that. Each person is to receive his own reward not according to the position he held but the way he worked at it.

Following are stories out of personal experience of a few whose names were never publicized but whose lives are remembered by those whose own lives they touched. Like some of Paul's fellow workers, the names are recorded only in the Book of Life.

THE PEPPERMINT MAN

Anton Justad was born in Norway on July 30, 1869. He emigrated to America as a young man settling in Concord, Massachusetts, for a brief time. While there he became acquainted with Dr. L. J. Pederson, then pastor of the Norwegian Evangelical Free Church of Boston. After a trip back to Norway to bring his bride to America, he went to Minneapolis and set up a dry goods store which he maintained for thirty-five years until his death in 1946.

In the summer of 1909 he was instrumental in bringing L. J. Pedersen to the city to preach in a tent to Norwegian and Danish immigrants. As a result, several were converted and others, already believers, were brought together. Twenty-four of those believers organized a congregation in November. Among the incorporators was my own father. At the constitutional meeting, Justad was elected Sunday School superintendent. Personally, I knew no other superintendent until my late teens. He did not know much about pedagogy but he knew the Word of God and children. His service to the local church and the denomination was not confined to the Sunday School. For many years he was a member of the Executive Committee of the Seminary and a trustee of the Norwegian-Danish Evangelical Free Church Association. He was also a member of the committee which erected the dormitory on the Minneapolis campus in the 1920s. The denominational paper, *The Evangelist,* wrote of him following his death, "He always held positions of trust in the local church as well as in connection with the Seminary and Bible Institute."

As a child, I always knew that when he would be called upon to make some remarks in the service that an offering was soon to follow. In a church hard pressed for funds, special appeals come often and it was his repeated assignment to make a plea for the offering.

His primary interest, however, was in the children and youth. He persuaded the congregation to permit services in English in the lower level of the building during the morning services which were in Norwegian. He assumed the responsibility for having speakers present. As a merchant he had become acquainted with many men and women whom he could call upon. As a teenager (see Chapter I) I was asked to lead those meetings. He never sought the spotlight. He would rather see young men and women develop their talents.

But it was as the peppermint candy man that I first learned to know him. All the children soon found out that if they got his attention he would pat them on the head and say, "God bless you," naming the child as he did so. Then he would reach into his pocket and take out a piece of originally white, unwrapped peppermints about the size of three stacked five cent pieces. They were sometimes a little grey but that was before we knew about bacteria! While others may have pointed a finger at the unruly "kids," his hand was outstretched to touch them.

I remember the occasion of my first violin solo at a children's program. My teacher, a member of the church, had tuned the instrument and left it out on the piano. However, some of my companions got to it and loosened the strings. I started to play not knowing that all four strings were loose. I tried my best to tune it but in a nervous state could neither see the people nor hear the sound. I stopped half way through the selection, marched back to the pew, completely humiliated while the boys snickered. The piece I was to play was most appropriate—"The Last Rose of Summer"—and that was not only the last rose but the first and last attempt to play a solo, though I did play later in the school orchestra and the church "stringband." After the program, Justad intercepted me in my attempted flight from humanity. There was the same pat on the head, the same "God bless you, Arnold," and the peppermint candy with an added word of encouragement.

Nearing the completion of high school at the Free Church Academy I felt it was time to look for some employment. Up to that time I had been sort of self-employed by delivering newspapers (a daily paper in Norwegian!), shining shoes on Saturdays and distributing weekly handbills for a local grocery store on Thursdays. The pay for that was fifty cents a Thursday but that covered streetcar fare to and from school for the week. To whom should I turn for help? Of course, the peppermint man. Mr. Justad said, "You go to the Northwestern National Bank and ask to see Mr. Clarence Hill, one of the vice presidents, and tell him you need a job and that Anton Justad had sent you." This, of course, was not the proper procedure. One should go to the personnel department, fill out proper forms, be interviewed and wait to be called. I did not know better than to go directly to the office of the vice president as instructed by Mr. Justad. Mr. Hill said, upon my getting up enough courage to call upon him, "How is Mr. Justad? I know him well. He is a fine Christian." From that moment on, Justad was no longer the peppermint man but one who had a good reputation, stature and influence in the business community as well as in the church. I got a job as bank messenger and worked hard to please the man who had taken on another dimension as a hero. After eighteen months, I returned to school and completed the Academy courses as well as four years of seminary work fully aware that my benefactor was also on the board of the school. That was also a source of comfort and inspiration.

During the first eighteen years as a pastor, no matter how busy I was during visits to Minneapolis, I would call on him in his store. Though failing in health toward the end of his life, his interest in the Free Church work never diminished. He always had many questions and comments. Why did I visit him? No, it was not to get a piece of peppermint candy but to hear him say each time as we shook hands on my departure, "God bless you Arnold, I pray for you every day." That is what I wanted and needed to hear. What a benediction! Heroes never know it.

HE NEVER MADE DEACON!

My first impression of this man was in itself an unforgettable experience. I had heard my parents say that he was back from the war (World War I) where he had served as an ambulance driver in England and on the continent.

There he stood on the steps of our church, straight as a soldier should stand, resplendent in his uniform; but the boys had eyes only for his highly polished leather leggings! I had seen thousands of soldiers march in a parade in Minneapolis as the Rainbow Division returned, but they had only ordinary, khaki, spirally wrapped cloth puttees.

This was something special and through the more than fifty years which have followed, the man in those leather leggings proved himself to be someone special to many people.

He never did see a gap between the spiritual and the secular. So, in the eyes of fellow members of the church, he was considered too practical to be really spiritual. I can still see him in dirty clothes, with soot all over his hands and face, as he was trying to get the fire going in the furnace on a Sunday morning while the deacons were in the study praying for fire in the pulpit. He believed that fire in the pulpit could not revive frozen corpses in the pew.

He knew that singing "Showers of Blessing" did not harmonize with the noise of dripping from leaks in the ceiling;

so while some looked in the hymnal, he was on the roof looking for the leaks.

When negotiations were under way for the purchase of another church building, negotiations which he initiated, he took us boys to inspect the building, long closed and in need of many repairs. He did not show us first the 1,200-seat sanctuary, but rather led us through the dark labyrinth in the basement from one room to the other which could be seen only with the inadequate beam of a flashlight. We expected a ghost any moment!

The visit became an adventure and right there he planted a dream in the minds of the boys as he pointed out a room filled with debris which they might some day fix up as their very own clubroom. This he said at a time when to suggest a club in a church bordered on heresy. With his guidance and our hard work, the dream came true.

I was in his Sunday School class for several years. Here, too, he was considered by some to be too practical to be spiritual. He sometimes prepared his class for Sunday's lesson by taking us on watermelon feeds and wiener roasts on Saturday. He held our attention on Sunday as he made use of his Bible school training in teaching the lesson, but embellished the truth with fascinating stories out of his own experience. For example, he was one of the first to fly as a passenger on a commercial flight, and for a long time afterward carried in his pocket the small salt and pepper shakers as an introduction to his own version of "show and tell." From that point on there was no end to illustrations.

At the Sunday School picnics he would not be asked to lead in the devotions, but he was on hand to give out the prizes for the contests which he often planned and supervised.

He had no separate compartments for the secular and the spiritual. He never made deacon! But whenever the church building was in need of repairs or business matters were in need of untangling, the congregation turned to him. Somehow, the church then, as now, overlooked the fact that those elected to serve at the tables had to meet the same spiritual qualifications as those who gave themselves to prayer and the ministry of the Word.

As the years went on he said little about his "home over there," but in the pocket of the coat he was wearing on his death was a copy of his will and other essential papers as well as instructions for his burial. On a trip to Minneapolis the previous year he had made arrangements with a local undertaker to take care of his burial upon his death, no matter where that might occur. He also discussed with the Secretary of Stewardship for the denomination how his estate might best serve the Lord upon his departure.

Yes, he was someone special.

He also refused to accept the idea of a generation gap. Every sleigh ride, toboggan slide, skating party and canoe trip involved him as planner, host or chaperone, and sometimes even as defender. For some years he owned a large home in the city, not only as an income producing investment, but as a place where he might entertain people, especially the young people.

He was a bachelor, and so adopted not only his many nieces and nephews in the United States and Norway but the children, grandchildren, and even great grandchildren of the fellow members of the church. He kept track of them all and stopped in to see them whenever in a particular area.

In my own travels I have often heard from some of these, "I bet you can't guess who dropped in to see us?"

That was easy.

I usually guessed right on the first try.

He brought a gift that could not be wrapped in paper and ribbon, as he brought news of people, places and happenings. He asked no favors except the privilege of helping with the dishes or taking the children on an excursion.

He inspired a reconsideration of our inheritance—how unique is the fellowship in Christ and the friendships it creates that extend to the children and the children's children. He never broke that link.

In Norway he had established a fund, the income from which upon his death would annually provide Christmas gifts for the Sunday School children in his birthplace. He kept contacts with the children of those who befriended him in England and on the continent during World War I. He took particular pride in following the boys from his Sunday School classes and boys' club. Once, when calling on my own family to check and see that my wife and children were making out all right while I was overseas in World War II, our younger son even suggested that he stay and be his daddy until his real daddy returned.

He never owned a car until his retirement, and then he bought a small station wagon which might serve as a mobile home. He even had curtains with a fringe, not on top, but on the botton.

I spotted him in the audience at a district conference in Florida and am so pleased now that I was moved to have him stand while I paid tribute to his influence not only on my own life but on the lives of many others for whom he had made Christianity a real, practical and normal excitement-filled life.

He was someone special.

His nephew said, "I have had nine uncles. I judge a man's wealth by the friends he has made. My Uncle Tom was the richest uncle of them all."

The man in the leather leggings will not attend any more conferences, nor will he visit or call on his friends. For on November 24, 1969, Tom B. Lahne, seventy-nine, dropped dead on the platform in Grand Central Station, New York, while changing trains as he was returning to his temporary residence in Bronxville after visiting friends in Orange, NJ.

In accordance with his instructions, the remains were brought to Minneapolis where they were laid to rest in the Fort Snelling Military Cemetery.

(Written following his death and published in the

Evangelical Beacon and subsequently in other religious periodicals.)

A HEART AS BIG AS THE MAN

J. Richard Johnson knew that his friends looked upon him as a hero long before he finished his work on earth; but he never fully realized the manner in which he was a hero to me from the very day I was installed as president of the merged Evangelical Free Church in 1952. To share that is the chief purpose of this story. However, the full impact cannot be experienced unless we also go back further in the history of the church and the life of this remarkable personality.

Born in Sweden in 1879, he emigrated to America with his parents in 1889 and settled in Rockford, Illinois. He had completed two years of public education following his arrival at the age of ten. At twelve he had to leave school to seek employment which he found at a stocking factory where he earned fifty cents a week for six twelve-hour days. A career followed as an inventor, designer and builder of heavy machine tools—mostly milling machines. He joined the Ingersoll Milling Machine Company in 1897 and had been at work on the day he died in 1956. He often said, "Looks like this is going to be a steady job."

Like many of his fellow immigrants, he was converted in one of the revivals of those early days in the history of the Evangelical Free Churches. We are fortunate in having the story of his conversion as told by a man who spoke to him about accepting Christ as Savior and who later served with him on the School Board for twenty-five years:

> It was in the month of January, 1903, and in days of glorious revival in that church, when sinners in large numbers, under deep conviction of sin, sought and found salvation. And it happened in one of those unforgettable after-meetings, which never could be limited as to the time element. Not so seldom, the midnight hour was approaching before some of those memorable meetings terminated.

The young flaming pastor-evangelist Gustaf F. Johnson had concluded his God-given message that evening. His "amen" was then, as always, the signal for us young believers to go forth in quest for souls. At the same time there were also groups of prayer warriors on their knees seeking God in behalf of unconverted loved ones and friends.

In the middle section of the church, right by the aisle, I saw a handsome young man. I knew that he was not a Christian. Should I approach him and invite him to the Savior? And how should I go about it? I realized even then, as a young inexperienced believer, that personal soul-winning was a mighty serious business. It required something more than "holy boldness." Sanctified common sense was equally important. In my heart I earnestly prayed for grace and wisdom in dealing with this particular case. I soon found out that many words were not necessary to convince him of his need of Christ as Savior. Convicted by the Holy Spirit, he yielded to Him. Humbly he took his place before God on his knees. Honestly and sincerely he prayed, then trusted in the Lord for the rest. And so a new name was written down in glory. It was Richard Johnson's great hour of decision. Saved by grace, through faith in Christ, he began to live by faith. And there was never a turning back to the old life. In his new-found life, new vistas of opportunities opened up to him—opportunities of precious fellowship with the people of God and of exalted service unto his Lord and to his fellow men.

That the Free Church of Rockford, where he through the many years was a most loyal and highly esteemed member, should benefit greatly by his valuable service and generous support, seems quite natural. But in his Christian activities he reached out into many fields of missionary endeavor, at home and abroad.[1]

His son wrote, "Apart from my father's love for his family, the local church and the Evangelical Free Church, his big interests were the Trinity School, the Swedish American Hospital, and the Ingersoll Milling Machine Company. The day he died, he spent the morning at a board meeting of the hospital of which he had been chairman for twelve years. The afternoon was spent at the factory from which he called me and also my brother-in-law asking us to come over to his home after dinner. His purpose was to sell us tickets for a hospital benefit concert. He died in my arms about 9:15 that evening. Talk about working up to the last minute!"

His support went far beyond words and even beyond monetary support. He even put his future needs on the line for the Free Church School. In the early 1930s the school was at the point of bankruptcy. The bank had started foreclosure proceedings on the main building. Johnson did not have cash available to save the building so he used his life insurance to refinance the mortgage. This involved about $15,000 for which he held notes. At an annual meeting in Holdredge, Nebraska, he cancelled half of the notes and the other half a year later. Pastor Frank W. Anderson in the tribute quoted earlier, concluded, "I shall never forget the way he used to pray at our board meetings. There could be no doubt as to his sincerity and his great sense of reverence as well as his childlike faith when he approached the Holy One. Hearing him speak to God for men, no one could escape the impression that he was in actual contact with heaven."

While the Evangelical Free Church of America has been blessed with many generous supporters throughout its first century, Johnson's faith in the future of the school as expressed in his move to save the building was most unusual.

Personally, however, as I told the family and other friends at the dedication of the Johnson Hall (dormitory) on the Trinity Campus in 1968, he was an unsung hero in an entirely different dimension. It happened at Winona Lake, Indiana, on the evening of June 29, 1952, when I was installed as president. It was a meeting filled with emotion as my predecessor, E. A. Halleen, gave the charge and Pastor Elmer Johnson offered a prayer of consecration while a large preacher's chorus standing behind us sang softly:

All to Jesus, I surrender,
All to Him I freely give;
I will ever love and trust Him,
In His presence daily live.

All to Jesus I surrender,
Lord, I give myself to thee;
Fill me with thy love and power,
Let thy blessing fall on me.

But that was not the end of that unforgettable experience. As Halleen and I walked off the platform, Johnson was hurrying as fast as the crowd and his stiff leg and cane (he suffered from a "dry socket" hip) would permit him and reached us as we came down the last step from the platform. He embraced Halleen and poured out words of thanks to him for his leadership. As he commented on the joy of working with him in so many ways over so many years, I felt smaller and smaller. Should I stay or walk away? I didn't think he even remembered I was there. I moved a few steps away, for this was a sacred moment for these two giants and to them alone. Abruptly, he turned from Halleen to me, placed his hands on my shoulders with the cane down my back and said, "I have stood behind that man throughout all the years he has been our leader. Now I am transferring that loyalty, those prayers and support to you as our new leader. I love him and I love you. I will never let you down."

Whatever doubts I had about the future disappeared at that moment. With support like that how can you lose? One would wish that those who live only in the past, whose loyalty is only to the leaders of the past, who seem to act as though all the future in behind us could be possessed with the dedication to the cause of Christ through His Church as was J. Richard Johnson. In his act of commitment to the new leadership he was to me a hero who did not know it.

SHE WALKED THE SECOND MILE

Kristine Olsen was a charming, gracious, unobtrusive, soft-spoken little lady easily lost in a room filled with people. She would have been surprised and embarrassed if she had been told prior to her homegoing thirty years ago (1953) that the story of her life would be considered worthy of a section in this book even under the heading of unsung heroes. As far as I know, she never held a position of leadership in the women's organization of the church. First, she was too busy supporting her four children and second, she just wasn't the type that either seeks or is chosen for leadership. However, in her own way, she was an entrepreneur. Upon emigrating from Norway she and her husband and two small children settled on Staten Island, New York. Most of the immigrants including Mr. Olsen found employment in the numerous shipyards as ship carpenters. The Olsens were not in America very many years before the husband and father died, leaving the widow with two sons and two daughters, ranging from two to twelve years of age. What was she to do now alone in a strange land, possessing no special skills, knowing little English and at a time when there were few opportunities for employment available to women? If there had been, what could have been done about day care for the four children? There was one thing in which she had experience in addition to caring for small children and that was cooking. So she decided to take in boarders. There were many single men working as carpenters in the nearby shipyards. These were also Norwegian immigrants so there was no problem in communication. Then there were meals like those their mothers had served in the old country adding a bit of nostalgia to each meal. As World War I broke out there were many shipyards and an influx of more immigrant workers gravitating to Staten Island. Mrs. Olsen moved and rented a larger house nearer the larger shipyards and was able to serve as many as seventeen. By the time we arrived to assume the pastorate of the congregation she was able to enjoy a little leisure, the children now having reached adulthood and had families of their own.

Now to the story of the second mile. We arrived on the

Island in December of 1933. The preparations for our coming were well worked out. The committee completed the mile by planning the program, sending out invitations and publicizing the installation service of the new pastor in the local paper. The trustees had also performed their assigned duty by finding us an apartment, though the use of that name could be misleading. It consisted of two rooms on the second floor of a one family house.

We were brought there on Saturday evening. All those involved in the planning could now report they had done their duty—they had walked the mile required of them.

We looked the apartment over. There was an old fashioned ice box at the head of the stairs but nothing in it. There was a small room over part of the stairway containing a table and a small cupboard. We wondered what we would do for breakfast. If there were restaurants nearby we had no way of knowing. Without a car there was no way of looking for a store. Complicating the problem even further was the fact that our cooking utensils, dishes, etc., as well as most of our clothing and all our books had been shipped via the railroad and didn't arrive until two months later. Naturally we were crestfallen.

Then we opened one of the two cupboard doors. There was a bag containing coffee, sweetrolls, a can of milk, sugar and coffee cake. Our drooping spirits soared. There was everything we needed for an evening snack and the next morning's breakfast. We borrowed a coffee pot, can opener, dishes, and spoons, knives, and forks and had our first little party in the new home—our first.

No one asked us if we had found the bag of groceries. It was several months before we discovered who had gone beyond the call of duty; who had walked the second mile. You guessed it! It was Kristine Olsen. Being related to the owner of the house, she was able to borrow a key. She walked several blocks to a store (she had no car) and carried the groceries to the house, secretly placing the bag in the cupboard. As we learned to know her better, we found this was her life style. Call it extrasensory perception or whatever you choose but she had an uncanny ability to sense a need. Several times she called on us at times when we needed some help in ways others would never consider important but that were important to us.

Jesus said about the woman who performed a service others had overlooked, "Wheresoever this gospel shall be preached in the whole world, there shall also this, that this woman hath done, be told for a memorial of her" (Matt. 26:13).

BEYOND HER ABILITY

It was while flipping the pages of the April 29, 1925, issue of the Norwegian denominational paper, *Evangelisten,* that I came upon a picture of a group of students at the Evangelical Free Church School which brought to mind the story of Malena Svalheim.

The accompanying article explained that the students in the photograph were those who were preparing themselves for work on the mission fields overseas. It was interesting, over half a century later, to reminisce as to just how accurate those predictions had been. All had eventually entered Christian work though not all on fields abroad. One served as a pastor in Norway and later as superintendent of a nursing home in the United States, two served in Russia, three in China, one in Africa, one in South America, two served in India, one as a pastor's wife in Norway and two served as pastors in the United States. One of these later spent several years as a professor at Trinity. One of the missionaries to China eventually returned to his native land, Denmark, and served for several years as the head of a sister denomination in that country.

The prediction in the article regarding future plans were conspicuous by one omission. Although Malena Svalheim was identified as one of those in the picture there was not a word about her in the text. That omission was not an oversight. Though she would say, when asked, that she planned to go to Africa as a missionary, not even the teacher who wrote the story seemed to think she would ever reach the field, for if there ever was a most seemingly unqualified candidate she was it.

Important as are a sense of calling, dedication and determination for anyone, and she had those, schools and mission boards must look for additional signs.

She was born in Norway, April 6, 1899, to a family of modest wealth and spent her earliest childhood on a large farm. Her mother died in Miss Svalheim's childhood. Her father later remarried and purchased a large farm near Drammen. She and her brother inherited an estate from a grandmother which provided funds for her trip to America and the three-year attendance at the school.

She came directly from Norway to the school in Minneapolis and soon gravitated to the bottom of every class. This was due to a combination of difficulty with the English language and being a slow learner. Finally, rather than drop her as a student, she was encouraged to attend classes taught in English merely as an auditor. One classmate recalled her as "shy and an introvert." Another recalled, "I know she was not a bright student." She was inconspicuous even in a small crowd. I am also reminded of what Abba Eban wrote in his autobiography about Lord Balfour's niece—"a lady of strong character, awkward of movement, embarrassingly deficient in feminine attraction but exquisitely subtle in perception."[2] However, I was to discover nearly twenty-five years later the paradox that behind that reserve was a self-willed, self-reliant, independent, rugged individualist possessed with a passion for missions.

I had lost track of her when she returned to Norway after failing to be accepted as a candidate for Africa by a mission board. Imagine my surprise when visiting the mission field in Swaziland, South Africa, in the 1950s to find Malena Svalheim working with the Misses Oddveig Thompson and Dagny Iverson at one of the stations.[3] Apparently I couldn't hide my curiosity and the other two workers on the station explained that Miss Svalheim inherited a sizeable estate in Norway and with the help of others worked out a plan whereby the estate would insure regular support. This was her second inheritance and one large enough to support her the rest of her natural life no matter where she lived. It came from the estate of an uncle, one of Norway's prominent citizens who served as president of the lower house in that nation's parliament (Stortinget). She went to Africa in 1928 at her own expense. The support was forwarded through The Evangelical Alliance Mission in America which provided her with missionary credentials. When World War II broke out it was no longer possible to send funds out of Norway. The Lord stepped into the breach and led the Olivet Evangelical Free Church of Muskegon, Michigan, to meet her financial needs until her death in April of 1958, following a lingering illness at the Mosvold Mission Hospital in the T.E.A.M.[4] field in South Africa. Her sister, a nurse and also a missionary, cared for her those last eight months. "I was," she wrote, "to see the deep love the people had for her as every day some came to visit and pray with her."

What could she do? I found her cooking and keeping house for two women missionaries, thus releasing them from chores which would greatly diminish the time they could give to evangelism and teaching. She had acquired a radiance which revealed an inner joy over a dream come true. One also got the feeling she was saying, "I told you so!"

One missionary who was on the field during Svalheim's tenure remembers: "She was almost a second Malla Moe,[5] only lacking in leadership qualities which Miss Moe had. Malena spent many weeks at a time out among the nationals. She was greatly loved and I recall one time when she returned how amazed she was at the way God had worked. She didn't realize she had been the instrument. When Malena was at home at the mission station she was something like Miss Thompson's 'good man Friday.' She loved to work in the fields superintending the work of the school children and seeing that the animals (they had some cows) were well taken care of. I would certainly feel that Malena was an unsung hero."

Another co-worker wrote: "Miss Svalheim loved Africa and the Africans. I know she was interested in the soul winning ministry and she, like other missionaries, went often out to the field to witness for the Lord, sleeping in the "bush" like the others. Of course, Miss Thompson had gifts which Miss Svalheim did not have but I am sure they shared responsibilities as faithful fellow workers."

A third missionary who recalled her from the days on the field wrote: "At the Esinceni Mission Station there were many children. They carried on an extensive agricutural program. Miss Svalheim was right at home in farm work and assisted in the work and proved to be a capable teacher. In everything she did she proved to be a faithful and sincere Christian." She was well aware of her limitations which is a desirable trait, especially among those serving the Lord. The correspondent continued: "She was one of the quiet ones—said little but listened much and made her own decisions. My best remembered experience was during a visit to Esinceni. We were gathered for a Sunday dinner. Miss Svalheim had just returned from a week of meetings at an out-station. Among other experiences, she shared the Word at a Thursday meeting at a school. Following her testimony, several stood and said, 'I choose Jesus.' There was much weeping, and confession of sin. Several of the believers also confessed sins in the spirit of repentance. 'I couldn't explain what happened,' she concluded, 'except that the Spirit of God came over us. It certainly could not have been the result of something I said.' "

It happens often that those who are willing to use whatever talent they may have soon find those talents multiplied. A beautiful tribute is paid to her work by her sister who wrote, "Malena could be out for days or maybe weeks visiting the *Kraals* together with the women of the church. She would often go out together with Malla Moe and give out the Gospel. She was used to walking in the mountains of Norway, and there are plenty of hills around Esinceni and there are people living everywhere. I came to Esinceni to work with Miss Thompson while Malena was on furlough. Because of my sister I was received with open arms and hearts by the people there and had a glorious time walking in her footsteps . . . I am thankful to the Lord for the example she was to me as a soul winner. She worked with eternal values in view and did not care to be seen by the world."

Heroes never know it! A "loner" in life, many co-workers and Africans were present at her burial. Several spoke of her faithful service to her Lord. One woman said with tears, "She gave us the Gospel." The professor who failed to report her plans in 1925 is in for a surprise when the books of heaven are opened!

I carried with me from Zululand a deeper understanding of what Paul wrote about the believers in Macedonia:

> Moreover, brethren, we do you to wit of the grace of God bestowed on the churches of Macedonia; How that in a great trial of affliction the abundance of their joy and their deep poverty abounded unto the riches of their liberality. For to their power, I bear record, yea, and beyond their power they were willing of themselves; . . .
>
> (II Corinthians 8:1-3 KJV)

> For I testify that according to their ability and beyond their ability they gave of their own accord. (ASV)

> For I testify that they gave as much as they were able, and even beyond their ability. Entirely on their own, they urgently pleaded with us for the privilege of sharing in this service to the saints. (also vs. 4 NIV)

HE MOPPED THE FLOORS

"What does Kasper do around here?" asked one man at the congregational meeting when the members were trying to solve the dilemma of maintaining the building so large that it called for a corps of custodians while the church could not even afford to hire one. The man raising the question was one who worked with his voice rather than his hands. He was like those who in the time of Jesus loved to "pray standing in the synagogues and in the corner of the streets, that they might be seen of men" (Matt. 6:4). Jesus warned against sounding a trumpet when giving alms to be seen of men (Matt. 6:2). The critic blew his trumpet in two ways. First, by directly calling attention to his contributions and second by contrasting his work with the lack of work by others. Kasper was a man of few words and, true to his pattern, answered not a word.

But we must go back and take a closer look at Kasper to fully appreciate his heroism. Born to a family with extensive landholdings in Magnor, Norway, he was destined to have his future clouded along with those of his three brothers and one sister who were to share in the large estate occupied by a number of tenant farmers. His father became a gambler and an alcoholic besides being a soft touch for his tenants. He loaned them money which was not always repaid. The estate was squandered. He spent the rest of his days operating a one-horse dray service, picking up freight at the railroad station and delivering it to the stores in the town. Kasper found employment at the glass factory in the village (Magnor Glas) as an apprentice glassblower. The factory continues to produce some of the finest glass products in the world. However, he was much older than the other new employees and it would be a long time before he would be accepted as a senior glassblower.

He made two decisions which were to change the direction of his life. There was a revival in his community and in attending the services he accepted Christ as his Savior and Lord. A man of peace, he nevertheless remained faithful in his attendance at the State (Lutheran) Church at the "Hoi Messe" (high mass) on Sunday mornings but joined the other new believers to pray, study the Word, and share experiences in the prayer chapel on Sunday afternoons. He also served as Sunday School superintendent at the chapel.

The second decision was to emigrate to America. The four brothers agreed to do so in the following manner. The oldest would go first and save up enough money to pay for the passage of the second (Kasper) and the two together would provide passage money for the third. When the three were ready to send for the fourth, the father reneged, wishing to keep at least one son near him, a wish which all four sons respected. This procedure was quite common in those days. Kasper joined his brother in Minneapolis but was soon on his way to northern Minnesota to a job clearing land. He first sought a church and found a kindred spirit in the Swedish Mission Church.

In the meantime a young girl, who was a *seterjente* (dairy maid) herding the cattle on the hillsides of the mountain slopes of southern Norway, was converted in another revival. She traveled alone at the young age of sixteen to the same town in Minnesota because an older brother had already homesteaded there. Kasper, by then past thirty years of age, noticed her in the stringband. Both moved to Minneapolis and married a year later (1909). They first attended the Swedish Evangelical Free Church, attracted by the hospitality, the mighty preaching of E. A. Halleen during a time of revival, and the use of the Scandinavian language. Since his childhood home was close to the Swedish borde where he associated with Swedish young people, Kasper spoke Swedish as readily as Norwegian. Having attended the Swedish Mission Church in northern Minnesota and the Swedish Free Church in Minneapolis, he spoke often of the need for a merger of the Swedish Covenant, Swedish Evangelical Free and the Norwegian-Danish Evangelical Free Churches. The failure of the latter two to merge at the first attempt was a source of disgust as well as disappointment. He never lived to see his dream come true.

It was natural that when tent meetings in Norwegian

were held in the summer of 1909 Kasper and his wife would attend and become charter members of the new Norwegian-Danish Evangelical Free Church (see the story of the *Peppermint Man*). This was a decision which would contribute to the future history of both the Norwegian-Danish and Swedish denominations! Kasper became one of the signers of a call to would-be members to a formal meeting for the purpose of organizing a congregation and voting to purchase a church building. Having obtained employment with the Milwaukee Road together with his older brother, his roots were now transplanted into new soil.

From then on Kapser had five sources of pride—his family, the local church, the Evangelical Free Church of America, the Milwaukee Railroad and his American citizenship which he sought as soon as he qualified.

As to the railroad, one got the impression that it could not operate without his input. In that he was a prophet for the Milwaukee Road went bankrupt a few years after he retired! His interest in the church was evident to his last day. Even though dying, he asked about the health of one of the leading pastors (N. W. Nelson) who was ill at the time. He may sometimes have had misgivings about some pastors but he never permitted any derogatory remarks in his home about the church or the pastor.

The church grew rapidly as a result of the large influx of Norwegian immigrants and a continuous revival. After a few years, the building had to be enlarged by digging under the chapel to construct a basement for additional Sunday School space. Eventually, it was again too small, so the congregation purchased a large unused church building with an auditorium seating twelve hundred persons and a chapel seating an additional four hundred. In retrospect, the pioneers had to admit it was not a great leap forward. As stated at the beginning, the cost of maintenance added to the mortgage payments was exorbitant.

It was then that Kasper decided to offer his services privately to the chairman of the board of trustees to donate the kind of labor which he knew best. He was a humble coach cleaner for the railroad on the famous Hiawatha trains. Every day he would vacuum the seats and mop the floors. He told the chairman not to worry about the floors of the chapel and the auditorium with its twelve hundred opera chairs. He would walk the twenty minutes over from work (he never owned a car) at the railroad yards on Fridays, doing a portion each week. It could be said of him as of the postmen, "Neither rain, nor sleet, nor snow, nor summer heat shall keep these couriers from their appointed rounds."

Few knew of his voluntary service. Others were home with their families for dinner at that hour. When finished he would take the long half-hour trolley ride to his home for a late supper.

One might imagine a group of boys sharing and boasting about the positions held or work done by their fathers in the church. The pastor's son could tell of his father's role, all the people who called on him for counsel, etc. The chairman's son could say that even the pastor had to take orders from his father. The song leader's son could tell how all his dad had to do was wave his arm and song would come from the people, whereas the pastor also waved his arms as he preached but there was no song from the congregation. The treasurer's son could tell how his father carried the money home, rolled the coins by the kitchen table and wrapped the bills. He could also boast that his dad knew the banker personally. Imagine the embarrassment of Kasper's son when he would reluctantly confess that his father merely mopped the floors.

However, as he mopped, undisturbed, he could pray for whoever might be sitting in each opera chair the following Sunday. As he mopped the floor in front of the platform, he could pray that many might kneel on the floor accepting Christ as Savior or committing their lives to the Lordship of

Jesus, or helping those responding to the invitation. It was, no doubt, a nostalgic time as well as he recalled the day he first knelt in the little prayer chapel in the old country to accept Christ as Savior and Lord and he surely thanked God for the new direction of his life from that moment on.

Kasper passed away on January 27, 1941. The church bulletin for the following Sunday was dedicated to his memory. Included was a poem in his honor written by L. J. Pedersen:

In love we think of those who've gone before,
Of those who dwell on sinful earth no more,
They walked with us in mingled joy and pain,
Now God has called them to eternal gain.

Our lives on earth like evening shadows fleet
And all our labors never are complete.
Our bark is frail, the billows often high,
We cannot fail, oh Lord, when Thou art nigh.

For service wrought we praise, oh God, Thy name.
We do not pray for honor nor for fame,
But grant us grace Thy blessed will to know,
And at Thy call, a willing heart to go.

For friends who lived and died, we thank Thee, Lord
For those who loved Thy people and Thy Word,
Help us, like them, in all to faithful be,
And so in life and death abide with Thee.

Tune: Abide with Me

Pedersen also preached at the morning service on the subject, "A Truly Good Man."

The bulletin stated, "In dedicating this bulletin to the memory of Brother Kasper Olson, we remember his sincere quiet life and treasure his memory . . . The evidence of the love everyone had for him was clearly seen by the large floral display and the many friends present at the memorial service. He will be missed, not only by the family but by all who knew him. Our church will miss him. He was a loyal member from the very beginning and a faithful friend."

He mopped the floor. This is what he knew best. He had a skill which he dedicated to the service of Christ. As in all such service, there are rewards. He rejoiced Sunday evenings as people knelt at the altar on the floor he had mopped. These included his own sons. I should know for Kasper Olson was my father.

FOOTNOTES—CHAPTER VI

1. Frank W. Anderson writing in the *Beacon*, April 10, 1956.
2. Eban, Abba, *An Autobiography*, Random House, New York, 1977, p.24.
3. Oddveig Thompson and Dogny Iverson, long-time workers in South Africa were supported by the congregations of the former Norwegian-Danish Evangelical Free Church Association.
4. TEAM—The Evangelical Alliance Mission.
5. Malla Moe was one of the best known and most unique pioneer missionaries to Swaziland. Her biography, *Malla Moe (Petra Malena)*, written by Maria Nilsen and Paul H. Sheets was published by TEAM in 1956.

INDEX

Mosvold Mission Hospital, 191
Muskegon, Church at, 191

National Association of Evangelicals, 140
Nelsen, N. W., 119, 196
Nelson, Fred, 93
Nelson, John, 119
North Park College, 27
Norton, Wilbur, 133
Nyvall, David, 27

Olsen, Kasper, 198
Olsen, Kristine, 186
Olsen, Tom, 119
Olson, Emil, 91
Olson, Louis, 106
Olsson, Karl, 19

Pedersen, L. J., 50
Pennock, Church at, 95
Peterson, Hannah V., 114
Phelps Center, Church at, 74, 91, 97
Pia Desideria, 31
Pietism, 29, 30
Ponca, Church at, 139
Princell, J. G., 5
Preachers Help Fund, 111
Program for Progress, 123
Prophesying Daughters, 86

Reader's Movement, 6, 31, 35
Revell, Fleming H., 91
Revolving Fund, 121

Salem Church, Chicago, 20, 27
Sande, Hans, 119
Sande, Ole, 119
Scandinavian Baptist Conference, 73
Sellevaag, Ivar, 133
Shareholders, 122
Sivrin, Hilma, 86
Sjoquist, S. J., 95
Social Concerns Committee, 57
Spener, Philip, 31, 32
Staten Island, Church at, 84
Stewardship, Department for, 123
Svalheim, Malena, 189
Swaziland, 190